Conspiracy
Theory

A Christian Evaluation
of a Taboo Subject

Conspiracy Theory

A CHRISTIAN EVALUATION
OF A TABOO SUBJECT

DOUG VAN DORN

Waters of Creation Publishing
Dacono, Colorado

Douglas Van Dorn (1970-)
© 2020
Waters of Creation Publishing
Dacono, Colorado

Unless otherwise noted, references are from the
English Standard Version (ESV) of the Bible.

Cover Design by Stephen Van Dorn

ISBN-13: 978-0-9862376-9-0 (Waters of Creation Publishing)

Table of ~~Contents~~

Other Books by Waters of Creation

Waters of Creation: A Biblical-Theological Study of Baptism (2009)
Galatians: A Supernatural Justification (2012)
Giants: Sons of the Gods (2013)
Covenant Theology: A Reformed Baptist Primer (2014)
From the Shadows to the Savior: Christ in the Old Testament (2015)
The Unseen Realm: Q & A Companion (2016)
Five Solas (2019)

Christ in All Scripture Series

Vol. 1. *Appearances of the Son of God Under the Old Testament* by John Owen (2019)

Vol. 2. *A Dissertation Concerning the Angel Who is Called the Redeemer and Other Select Passages* by Peter Allix (2020)

Vol. 3. *The Worship of the Lord Jesus Christ in the Old Testament* by Gerard De Gols (2020)

Vol. 4. *The Angel of the LORD In Early Jewish, Christian, and Reformation History,* a compilation of Allix, Owen, and De Gols (2020)

Vol. 5. *Christ in the Old Testament: Promised, Patterned, and Present* revised and expanded second edition of the previously titled: *From the Shadows to the Savior: Christ in the Old Testament* by Douglas Van Dorn (2020).

Vol. 6. *Jesus: Who, What, Where, When, Why?* by Douglas Van Dorn (coming soon)

For more information, articles, radio shows, and broadcasts go to: dougvandorn.com

Dedicated to:

All my fellow consp   iracy theorist friends
      (you know   who you are).
         You make   life fun and
           much more   exciting
              than it
          otherwise   might be
        More than   that,
      you are able to   think rationally
      While making   wise decisions
    in the midst of   a crazy world
That we all know   exists around us

<u>P R E F A C E</u>

Black Helicopters	Chemtrails	JFK	JFK Jr.
New World Order	Denver Airport	George Soros	Freemasonry
Jesus/Mary Magdalene	Princess Diana	Area 51	Men in Black
Flat Earth	Water Conspiracy	HAARP	Smithsonian Coverup
Police State	Global Warming	Fluoride	MKUltra
Vaccinations	Manchurian Candidate	Moon Landing	CIA
Rockefellers	False Flags	9/11	Illuminati
Deep State	Bohemian Grove	"Paul is Dead"	FEMA Camps
Sandy Hook	Clinton Body Count	Jeffery Epstein	Obama Birth
Time Travel	Reptilians & Greys	Nazi Bell	Surveillance
Bilderberg Group	Plum Island	Skinwalkers	Monsanto
Stanley Kubrick	Flying Saucers	Stolen Body of Jesus	Manimal
Military Industrial Complex	Antarctica Bases	Disney Movie Covers	Rothchilds

WELCOME TO THE AMAZING WORLD OF conspiracy theories. I feel like I should be writing this book from inside my top-secret, booby-trapped sterilized steel office, a low buzzing—like the sound of electricity, but not quite—echoing in my ears, adjacent to my bioengineered extraterrestrial super-bee mega-farm, located in the middle of a corn field in the middle of nowhere North Dakota. And Mulder and Scully should be walking in any minute...

Alas, it isn't *where* I'm writing it from (although, I will tell you it is a secret closet that some have called the entrance to Narnia), but *when* I'm writing it. Much of what is being written in this book is taking place in real-time, in the midst of the coronavirus (COVID 19) world-wide pandemic and specifically during what Q calls "10 days. Darkness." Or, what some of his anon-followers are calling "10 days of darkness," but which in the original post was actually spelled "10 days. Darnkess," which lead to its own fascinating bunny trail, but I digress.

I suppose I have to take a moment to explain what I mean by Q, for even at its peak, this remarkable, unique, and strange darkweb phenomenon is only known to a minority of the population. According to Wikipedia (at least at this moment, since it is liable to change at any time), that bastion of neutral, authoritative orthodoxy for pop-culture, "QAnon is a far-right conspiracy theory detailing a supposed secret plot by an alleged 'deep state' against U.S. President Donald Trump and his supporters." Nothing like good old astroturfing (see the last chapter for more on astroturfing) to take the edge off of an evil conspiracy theory. I found out about this wiki entry because *YouTube* makes sure that anyone watching any video associated with Q has this vital, unbiased bit of information just below every video posted, just to make sure that those watching know that what they are seeing cannot be trusted because it is coming from fringe, extreme, coocoo nutjobs. Thanks for that nannying, *YouTube*. It's so helpful to know that you have all my best interests at heart and that I'm not capable of thinking for myself without your omnipresent oversight.

According to the official *QResearch* page (as of April, 2020), "**Q Clearance Patriot**, more commonly known as **Q**, has tasked us with compiling events and evidence of the world-changing circumstances that have, and have yet to transpire." More specifically someone explains,

> Q first appeared in October 2017 on an anonymous online forum called 4Chan, posting messages that implied top-clearance knowledge of upcoming events. More than 3,000 messages later, Q has created a disturbing, multi-faceted portrait of a global crime syndicate that operates with impunity. Q's followers in the QAnon community faithfully analyze every detail of Q's drops … The mainstream media has published hundreds of articles attacking Q as an insane rightwing conspiracy, particularly after President Trump seemed to publicly confirm his connection to it.[1]

Q is surging in popularity at the present moment and has become the great conspiracy theory of our times (though it might be better to call it a PSYOP), in some ways enveloping a good many of the others under its sheltering wings. Here are a few things I see as reasons. First, Q is unlike anything else before it. It is an ongoing three-year drip of information coming from somewhere, and it sure seems like it is from a high-level source; it knows things it shouldn't be able to know if it were made up. Second, President Trump (and a few in the media) is playing along with it, either because it is real or for some other as of yet unknown reason. Third, it talks about some very dark things but provides "light at the end of the tunnel." The hope is contagious.

Finally, people are nervous and even scared about what they will see on the other side of this pandemic. Will it be life as normal? Almost no one thinks that. Will it end in a world-takeover, some kind of socialist dystopia with presidents, kings, senators, actors, and the media all in on the perfect conspiracy to destroy life as we know it and take all power to themselves? Perhaps there will be thousands of women and children suddenly show up who

---

[1] Deborah Franklin, "An Introduction to Q," *American Thinker* (Jan 14, 2020), https://www.americanthinker.com/articles/2020/01/an_introduction_to_q.html?fbclid=IwAR2ps d9Qpi8jRquEhGLI8FHcFi4CH-hjxyfN591u3292aQ94CTbYV1Pr4S0.

have been sold as sex-slaves in satanic ritual abuse (that's a Qanon theory). Maybe Jesus will come back? Or maybe it will be one of a dozen other theories. Or maybe it will be none of them.

All I know is that the present moment is probably the most fascinating (if not also disconcerting) thing I've ever lived through and many others echo the same. For that reason, I'll be using Q and some other conspiracy theories as kinds of living examples as we work our way through this book. The point is not to promote or denounce any of them. This book exists to help us think rationally and biblically about conspiracy theories, not to engage in them per se. So, their main purpose is to be illustrations for my higher target.

More to the point of this preface, I'll be doing this "live." That is, I'm not going to edit "after the fact" to make me look better. Fact is, I don't know what is going to happen, though I have an educated guess. I want this book to be helpful and I have a feeling that working this out myself can help both of us. For I am, like many of you, wondering how exactly a Christian should be thinking about conspiracy theories. What better way than to work through it myself? If I'm able to pull this off, whatever I end up writing needs to be timeless, for the topic at hand is a timeless issue, even if it is also at the present moment almost all-pervading in the hearts and minds of many people around the world.

My hope and prayer is that through my own reflections on these days and those of the recent past, I as a Christian and a pastor might be able to help someone struggling with how to think through in a rational and God-honoring way the taboo subject of conspiracy theories.

Doug Van Dorn
April, 2020

ORIGIN OF THIS BOOK

THIS BOOK HAS BEEN BREWING in my mind for nearly 15 years. I was talking to a friend, a fellow pastor, about how terribly sad 9-11 was and how great I thought George W. Bush handled it. Bush was still the president at the time. He said, "You're kidding, right?" That caught me off guard. "You do understand that he's the one that took those buildings down, right?" I was dumbfounded (and for the record, to this day I remain agnostic on exactly who it was that took down those towers). What in the world could make someone otherwise perfectly sane and in such a position of leadership say something as obviously absurd, no, dangerous, even treasonous as this?

But something about that comment took me back to that day. I was 31 years old. Our first-born child, a beautiful little girl, was just 9 days old. I was awoken, not by her early morning hunger cries, but by a phone call. It was sometime just after 8:00am Mountain Standard Time (I guess I was sleeping in a little). It was my father calling me from San Francisco. It was an hour earlier for him. He had been working on a big project for Ford Motor Company, and basically lived downtown for several months and he had been awake for a long time already.

"Turn on the television, now."

"Why?"

"Just turn it on."

I walked from our one-bedroomed apartment's sleeping quarters to the adjacent living room and found the remote. Then, as with everyone else who saw the images of that day, I was aghast. Not one, but both of the iconic World Trade Center towers were ablaze with dark, billowing, all-engulfing smoke. I rushed to get my wife, as I grabbed the newborn whom I had just woken up.

"You have to come in here."

"What is it?"

"You have to see this."

"What?"

"Just come and look." I wonder if my dad and I were the only two people who had no words to tell others. We knew that only the images could truly tell the story. Several minutes later, as I held that nine-day-old child in my arms, I watched as 417 meters of concrete and steel just imploded, falling in upon itself absolutely vertically in near free-fall speed.

Since I was a little kid, I had always wondered, how would they get a huge skyscraper down if it was in total disrepair? When I was 14, I had the great fortune to witness a controlled demolition. It was May 20, 1984, a Sunday, and we always went to church on the Lord's Day. But this Sunday, my dad asked if we would like to go to his office downtown for a once-in-a-lifetime opportunity. You see, he had a corner office on the 41st floor of Denver's iconic "Cash Register" building, and it had a perfect view of the Cosmopolitan Hotel, a 41-meter, twelve story piece of Colorado history built in 1926. That morning, they were going to take it down.

I recently re-watched that event that was forever etched into my teenaged mind. You can hear the countdown. 5 … 4 … 3 … 2 … 1. From the time of the first explosion to the building being entirely gone was about 8 seconds. The building itself was in a free-fall for about 5. Then it was over.

I distinctly remember thinking of that event during that moment I saw the World Trade Center tower, a building ten times the height of the Cosmo, fall to the ground in only a couple more seconds than it took the hotel. My thought was immediate. "Someone just blew up the World Trade Center." Then the other one fell the same way and as far as I was concerned, that was that.

And then.

And then I was told, like everyone else, that it was the failing beams over 100 stories up in the air, caused by jet-fuel weakening their molecular structure, that caused the towers to fall. That was the story. I believed it. Why shouldn't I? I live in the United States of America—government of the people, by the people, and for the people. This isn't the U.S.S.R. This isn't China. Our leaders only have our best intentions in mind. My immediate thought was quickly snuffed out by the "official story." Then, just a couple of months later, it was cemented by the President himself who said, "Let us never tolerate outrageous conspiracy theories concerning the attacks of September the 11th."[2]

It was at that moment, as my friend told me his crazy conspiracy theory, as I began reflecting on those older memories of personally watching the buildings fall, live, that a seed of doubt crept into my mind. *What if I was right? What if someone did take it down?* Now, let's just get this out of the way right now. This book is not interested in investigating the demise of the World Trade Center

---

[2] George W. Bush, "United States of America Statement at the 56th Session of the United Nations General Assembly" (Nov 10, 2001). It is interesting that our Dispatch blames the "Communists" for all conspiracy theories, while Bush blamed people "promoting the propaganda of terrorists." In other words, any other theory than the one set forth as "official" is put into the worst possible light.

towers. There has been plenty written and documented on that already from just about every perspective imaginable. Do your own investigation; come to your own conclusions. I won't fault anyone for any conclusion they come to if they do that.

Rather, what I'm interested in is the idea of, and let me say this explicitly with quotations marks, "conspiracy theories." I want to look at the subject itself and all that surrounds it. Here's another anecdote to reinforce why and to explain to you a little more of my own history on this. A few years after this conversation with my friend, I began to research a book on giants in the Bible. This research came about innocently enough. I was preaching through Exodus; I don't remember where I was exactly in that process. I know it was late in 2010, which has itself been ten years ago now.

Somehow, I came across a fascinating journal article in *Bibliotheca Sacra* by a scholar I had never heard of named Michael Heiser. His topic was at best tangentially related to what I was studying in Exodus. But it was an absolutely fascinating discussion of a textual variant found in Deuteronomy 32:8. So I read it. The variant is really quite important to one's reading, not only of this passage, but quite frankly, of the entire Old Testament. Curiously, that leads to its own conspiracy theory that I will tell you about in a later chapter. But I digress.

A few months later, while studying for a sermon later in Exodus, I came across a different article that reminded me of that earlier one I had read. Curiosity got the better of me and I wanted to know if there was any chance it was the same author. Unbelievably, it was! Coincidence? *Conspiracy?* I was hooked.

I started digging and found that Dr. Heiser has similar hobbies and interests to me. He likes the X-files, Coast-to-Coast radio, and the whole subject of extra-terrestrials. Strange hobbies for a pastor and a scholar, perhaps, but I promise you, we are not the only ones. Heiser even did conferences at Roswell during the annual UFO conventions there to do biblical apologetics to what I would say is in some ways an unreached people group--UFOlogists. Mike has since become a friend, but back in those days, almost no one knew who he was.

I quickly found that he was offering a book he was working on for free on his website. That book eventually became *The Unseen Realm* which I highly recommend you read (along with its *Q & A Companion* which I wrote to go along with it). In that book, I started reading about things I had never heard anyone, especially a scholar, talk about in public: gods, demons, giants, meeting places where the supernatural realm interacts with our realm, angels creating children with human women? In my circles, some of these are themselves considered conspiracy theories by not a few people.

It was compelling. Since I personally knew no one else I could talk to about this material, I decided to work it out in my own head by writing a book. That book developed in much more detail the giants introduced to me by Dr. Heiser. Prior to this, I had almost no knowledge of giants other than Goliath, but I quickly discovered that others had written about it. I also discovered that a lot of them were, let's just say, sensationalizing the topic and probably making some good coin doing it.

The sensationalism may be related to another "conspiracy theory," one in that field of study. It deals with the Smithsonian. The theory is premised on the truthful claims of the thousands of newspapers, magazines, local county diaries, and even state historical society write-ups on giant bones found throughout North America that we have on record. These appeared roughly between the years 1750-1950. But today we have almost no physical evidence that any of it ever happened. Why? The Smithsonian covered it up, took them all away, one by one, in secret under the ruse of overseeing archeological digs, to hide this truth from the public. My point here is, I can't seem to get away from the topic of conspiracy theories. Even if I'm not particularly looking for them, they seem to find me, as I'm sure they have found you too, as I'm guessing you otherwise would probably not be interested in this book.

"Conspiracy theories" are much more common than I think a lot of people want to admit. You can find them in almost any field of study, any area of culture, all forms of social interaction, and throughout all of history. There are almost infinite quantities of little conspiracy theories. Everyone has them in their families, businesses, government, schools, churches. A mother conspires against one kid because she prefers the other. A boss conspired with the secretary to steal secrets from his company. A teacher and principle conspired to hide their adulterous affair. A pastor conspired against the people by taking money from the offering plate. In all cases, someone else is covering for them. That's the conspiracy *theory*, and they make for great watercooler or family reunion gossip, don't they?

Of course, there are also big conspiracy theories as well. Again, I'm not particularly interested in this book in investigating any of those *per se*, even though I will be using a couple of them, particularly Q (see the Preface) as working illustrations as we move along. I'm not even really interested in figuring out which are real, and which are not. What I'm interested in this book is asking questions about them and helping Christians think through this fascinating, wide-spread, yet taboo subject that affects many of us but no one wants to talk about publicly.

Why do some people look at this phenomenon one way (avoiding, so they think, all conspiracy theories at any cost and publicly rebuking anyone they see engaging in them)? Why do others look at it a completely different way (entertaining almost any new theory that comes down the pike, sort of like Jerry Fletcher, Mel Gibson's character in the movie *Conspiracy*

Theory)? How is the phrase "conspiracy theory" being used in our day? Is there any kind of traceable origin to the phrase itself? Might that have anything to do with the way we process events when others throw that language around? What are we to make of conspiracy theories as Christians? Does the Bible teach us anything about them? Does it give us principles for how to think properly about them? Should we just avoid them altogether and not waste time writing books about the subject? (While there are a lot of books on conspiracy theories, very few Christians have written on this matter). What is the relationship of conspiracy theories to the realm of truth? What does it say about us if we entertain a conspiracy theory or if we absolutely refuse to think about them? Are there dangers in entertaining conspiracy theories? Are there dangers in not entertaining them? How can a person avoid what I call a "fractured mind" or various other horrors that can come because of them? How can we stay sane in a world full of conspiracies? All of these questions and more will be addressed in these pages.

It is probably important to wrap up this chapter by addressing the obvious question, who cares, or, at least, why should you care? The short answer is that this subject is entertained by and affects many more people than those not entertaining it can possibly imagine. That's the problem when a subject is not allowed to be taken seriously in public. It does not go away; it simply goes underground.

A longer but related answer is that we are living in the age of conspiracy theories. Unfortunately, no matter what happens with any one theory, whether it proves true or false, this isn't going to end. We have always had these with us, and they will not go away after we are gone. But at the present moment, this feels more acute than perhaps at many times in human history. Here I want to return to current events as I write this book as explained in the Preface.

When an event arises and questions immediately begin to crop up about the official narrative, people become confused. Those disturbed enough by the incongruity then go looking for other solutions, which I actually think is a healthy thing. This is all exacerbated when those events directly affect you, as is happening now with this coronavirus. In the midst of such times, when a dozen competing theories vie for the throne of truth in a person's mind, a real war is taking place. Should I believe "the official narrative?" Does X theory, Y theory, or Z theory make more sense?

Often times, these competing ideas can have some pretty devastating consequences on how we think about certain aspects of the world, of culture, of corporations, of politics and politicians, of a great many things. I believe, for example, that the hatred that so many have had for Obama and then, with the opposite people, Trump, can be explained at least in part to competing *public* narratives that are now vying for power in the public sphere. This is perhaps best exemplified best by President Trump's "fake news" meme which is embodied in our corporate public life in the divide we have between MSNBC and CNN on one side, and FOX News editorialists and Rush Limbaugh on the other. These are not unbiased sources of information (unfortunately, only one side of this usually admits it), and we do not have monolithic public agreement on "the facts." Though I think it is good and necessary for a republic to have disagreement, if many people think there used to be total agreement and if they also think we used to have pristine, unbiased, neutral reporting, but suddenly we don't, this can have some pretty damaging consequences, especially on how people think about and treat one another.

Given the implications of simply the pervasiveness of conspiracy theories, how is this not something that we should think about seriously? When so few people want to talk sanely about this subject, and yet it is literally a part of each one of our lives, whether we know it or not, I believe it is the duty of Christians to think well about these things for ourselves, so that we can help others think through the same thing.

Next, conspiracies exist. Not conspiracy theories, but conspiracies. They are real. While obsessing over them can do harm, and even entertaining them can have radical changes on a person's outlook on life, for better or for worse, not entertaining them can be just as harmful. When people absolutely refuse to entertain even the possibility of conspiracy, they fool themselves. I'm not talking about on every single issue; but on the level of the idea itself. Few were looking for a conspiracy from the Bolshevik Party in 1917 when Vladimir Lenin came to power. Fifty million people ended up dead from that oversight. The same holds true for the Armenian Genocide from 1914-1923, the Nazi movement of the 1920s or so many more. Prior to their taking place, you would have been considered a conspiracy theorist for even thinking that these revolutionaries had anything but your best interest at heart. Afterwards, we see the absolute devastation of human life that they left in their wake.

At the same time, the power of such grotesque human evil to create distrust can create an opposite kind of danger, one that can end up turning a person literally insane. But insanity, the kind of which is portrayed in Gibson's *Conspiracy Theory* or by Brad Pitt and Bruce Willis in *12 Monkeys* is but the last and greatest tragedy that some face from entering into this world of unknown darkness. Perhaps relatively minor, yet just as real personal impacts include worry, anxiety, fear, panic, paranoia, and many other emotional reactions that are detrimental to a life of peace in Christ.

For these reasons, I want to enter into this world of conspiracy theories, as much for my own sake as for yours. I believe that thinking clearly about this subject can be not only a help to us, but to others we know are struggling. I hope this book will help you think better about the unknown by helping you understand what conspiracy theories are, how they have always been with us, what good they can provide, what dangers surround them, and how you can navigate the minefields in which they lay.

Yet, at the end of the day, while some may lead you towards a truth and others may lead you away, there is only one truth that can help a person in both the most immediate and ultimate sense. That truth is knowing God, knowing that he is sovereign over all things and that, in Christ Jesus, he means you well. I'll hammer this truth home at the end. But until then, that doesn't mean we shouldn't also learn to think about conspiracy theories.

THE ORIGIN OF A PHRASE

WHAT IS A "CONSPIRACY THEORY"

W HAT IS A "CONSPIRACY THEORY?" There are two ways I want to unpack this question. The first is historical. The second is definitional.

The Historical Answer

What is the origin of the phrase "conspiracy theory?" Thanks to Google Books, we have access to information that helps us answer this question pretty easily. The phrase does not seem to have been used much prior to around 1870 where we find it being used in a courtroom trial. *Harpers Weekly* reported, "This was the end of the conspiracy theory; but it was an indication of the spirit and manner in which the defense was to be conducted."[3] In the *Journal of Mental Science* of the same year we read, "It was at least more plausible that the conspiracy theory of Mr. Charles Reade, and the precautionary measure suggested by Dr. Sankey of using a padded waistcoats in recent cases of mania with general paralysis—in which mental condition nearly all these cases under discussion were—seemed to him of practical value."[4] I would say that both of these uses are morally benign, though they are clearly not putting the opposition's viewpoint in a positive light. They are benign because they are not attacking anyone for having a conspiracy theory.

This benign, yet negative, use of the phrase continued long into the 20th century.[5] The point of this is, the phrase was used for many decades to speak to an alternative testimony of events, one that went against the grain of popular opinion of an "official" story. It was a view or theory with which some other person did not himself agree. Of course, in a court of law, it is part of the burden of proof to determine what really happened, and so an "official" story can't be had until after the trial is over. Outside of a lawcourt, however, things can be quite different.

For nearly 200 years in the United States, you had conspiracy theories being part and parcel of American life. As it regards politics, for example, one scholar explains,

> Not just a sideline to a mainstream politics of reasonable discussion and rational exchange, conspiracy thinking has long occupied a central place in American politics. America is, in fact, embedded in it. From the anti-Freemasonry and anti-Catholicism of colonial America, to the recurrent nativism of the

---

[3] "The Late Trial and Tragedy," *Harper's Weekly: A Journal of Civilization* (March 28, 1870), 338.

[4] "Psychological News," *The Journal of Mental Science*, ed. Henry Maudsley, and John Sibbald, vol XVI (London, J and A. Churchill, 1870-71), 141.

[5] See Katharina Thalmann, *The Stigmatization of Conspiracy Theory Since the 1950s: "A Plot to Make us Look Foolish"* (Routledge, 2019).

nineteenth century, to the McCarthyism and Cold War nucle-
arism of the twentieth century, major political movements in
the United States have been informed by fears of conspiracy as
well as by the actual need to engage in conspiracies to combat
threats to national sovereignty. Indeed, one might say that
conspiracy thinking produces America as a nation: it provides
narratives that tell Americans who 'we' are.[6]

Essentially, this can be applied to all of American life,

> During the Revolutionary War ... both the colonists and
> the British were convinced that the opposite party was en-
> gaged in a conspiracy, but on the American side, conspiracy
> theories helped to unite the economically, geographically,
> and ethnically very diverse and divided colonists ... [We
> must stress] both the prevalence and pivotal role of conspir-
> acy theorizing in American culture from the colonial era to
> the mid-20th century ... [There is] a great variety of conspir-
> acy theories, ranging from fears about Illuminati in the 18th
> century to fears of communism in the 1950s. Whether dur-
> ing the Salem witchcraft crisis, the presidency of John Ad-
> ams, to the late antebellum era, conspiracy theories shaped
> politics and history as they both stabilized communities by
> exaggerating and exploiting fears of a conspiratorial enemy
> said to threaten the group from without, and/or destabi-
> lized communities by exaggerating and exploiting differ-
> ence among community members.[7]

Finally, and very importantly, conspiracy theories were actually
something all educated, rational men engaged in.

> Conspiratorial interpretations—attributing events to the
> concerted designs of willful individuals—became a major

---

[6] Jodi Dean, "Declarations of Independence," *Cultural Studies & Political Theory*,
ed. Dean (Ithaca: Cornell UP, 2000), 291 [285-304].
[7] Thalmann, 8-9.

means by which educated men in the early modern period ordered and gave meaning to their political world. Far from being symptomatic of irrationality, this conspiratorial mode of explanation represented an enlightened stage in Western man's long struggle to comprehend his social reality. It flowed from the scientific promise of the Enlightenment and represented an effort … to hold men personally and morally responsible for their actions.[8]

In other words, this is anything but the fringe topic of lunatics that we find today. So what happened?

All this changed in 1967, at least, according to a conspiracy theory that is. You might call the information I'm about to tell you a conspiracy theory about "conspiracy theory." In fact, it has literally been called that. This ironically shows just how penetrating this phenomenon has gone into the modern world. I also think it is a good example of just how interesting and compelling these things can be.

At the heart, its claim is that the Central Intelligence Agency either invented (easily disprovable) or subverted and popularized the phrase "to disqualify those who questioned the official version of John F. Kennedy's assassination and doubted that his killer, Lee Harvey Oswald, acted alone."[9] The softer version, that it was subverted, is the one I want to look at here.

A CIA Dispatch from 1967 was released and made known to the public in 1976 when *The New York Times* requested it under the Freedom of Information Act, one of the truly great Acts in American history I might add. This CIA Document 1035-960 is titled, "Concerning Criticism of the Warren Report." The

---

[8] Gordon S. Wood, "Conspiracy and the Paranoid Style: Causality and Deceit in the Eighteenth Century," *The William and Mary Quarterly* 39:3 (July 1982), 411.
[9] Beth Daley, "There's A Conspiracy Theory That the CIA Invented the Term 'Conspiracy Theory' – Here's Why," *The Conversation* (March 16, 2020), https://theconversation.com/theres-a-conspiracy-theory-that-the-cia-invented-the-term-conspiracy-theory-heres-why-132117.

Warren Commission, you may recall, was established by President Lyndon Johnson on November 29, 1963, just a week after Kennedy was assassinated. The 888-page report, presented to President Johnson in September of 1964, became the official government story of the murder. Lee Harvey Oswald, a lone and crazed gunman, killed him. And that was that.

However, from the beginning, there were always skeptics of the official narrative, and not a few I might add. My own father recalls watching it and within hours thinking much like I did when the towers fell that something was off about what they were telling people. Of course, this event has been told and retold in books and movies and articles from every possible angle and perspective more times than there will be words in this book. The point here is this CIA document related to that terrible event.

"Concerning Criticism" was written, very deliberately, as a kind of CIA manual for how to deal with outside criticism of the Warren Investigation. The document is marked "PSYCH," meaning psychological operations, and has the stamp "CS COPY" meaning Clandestine Services Unit. This means it was a teacher's manual meant to disseminate its information to the wider public through the steps outlined in its pages. The things it says are quite revealing.[10]

For example, point 2. begins, "This trend of opinion is a matter of concern to the U.S. government, including our organization." What is this trend? "Speculation about the responsibility for his murder." Since when does the CIA get to care about what the American public thinks about the official stories coming out of Washington?

Point 2. concludes, "The aim of this dispatch is to provide material countering and discrediting the claims of the *conspiracy theorists*, so as to inhibit the circulation of such claims in other countries" (emphasis added). In the words of Rhodes

---

[10] For the full text, see Appendix 1.

Scholar finalist Richard Dolan, "In other words, the CIA is explicitly concerning itself with manipulating public opinion … The whole point is to create a silent propaganda system, posing as objective journalism, to manipulate what people think."[11]

One of the pieces of advice the Dispatch gives is found in point 3.a. "To discuss the publicity problem with liaison and friendly elite contacts (especially politicians and editors), pointing out that … the charges of the critics are without serious foundation, and that further speculative discussion only plays into the hands of the opposition. Point out also that parts of the conspiracy talk appear to be deliberately generated by Communist propagandists. Urge them to use their influence to discourage unfounded and irresponsible speculation." They actually use the language "elite contacts" and "propagandists." In other words, if possible, bury dissent. But if you can't do that? Use the elites.

Like who? The media, for example, or famous authors or celebrities. And what are they told to do? "Employ propaganda assets to refute the attacks of the critics." It is interesting that they actually call their own actions "propaganda." In those days, it was "book reviews and feature articles." These days, it is the internet, social media, search engine suppression, astroturfing, and so on. Or, you can use politicians. Perhaps this is not unlike Bush II telling the United Nations that amazing line we saw in Chapter 1, "Let us never tolerate outrageous conspiracy theories concerning the attacks of September the 11th." Give them their talking points. Tell them what to say as they disseminate the "correct" view to the masses. Why? Because all non-official speculation is "irresponsible." That's its language, not mine.

So that is the conspiracy theory behind "conspiracy theory." As I hope you can see, the theory certainly has some pretty

---

[11] Richard Dolan, "Managing Conspiracy Theories: How the CIA Created the Term," *YouTube* (May 4, 2019), https://www.youtube.com/watch?v=ES81R8ipzCw.

powerful points, points rooted in an actual CIA document that really was written to do these very things to the public. Frankly, this rather makes our own CIA look positively fascist (and I do not mean that as a pejorative, simply as truth). But it probably isn't quite that easy to explain the history. Rather than say that the CIA by this single propaganda campaign changed how the phrase is viewed forever, perhaps it is better to see it as a defining moment in a series of events that were sweeping through civilization at the time.

I'm opening up here the age-old problem of the chicken and the egg. I was a Marketing major in college and this question came up often. Does advertising (itself a form of propaganda, usually benign but never neutral) create cultural needs and wants (the chicken) or reflect them (the egg)? The true answer is that there is a synergism between these two things. Marketing both creates needs and wants (through new cultural memes) that were not there, while simultaneously reflecting those that are already there. The same is true of many things, including "conspiracy theory."

Scholars have demonstrated that it really was an entire series of events over the span of perhaps 20-30 years that really saw the phrase change.[12] But now I want to discuss what the change did to the phrase. I've hinted at it already, but perhaps now it is best to introduce the second way to think about our question. Let's think about a definition of "conspiracy theory."

The Definitional Answer

The phrase comes from two separate words. The first, "conspiracy," is defined by the modern Webster's Dictionary as, "The Act of conspiring together." That's not terribly helpful, but the much older famous 1828 edition written by Noah Webster himself is. "A combination of men for an evil purpose; an agreement between two or

---

[12] See Thalmann.

more persons, to commit some crime in concert; particularly, a combination to commit treason, or excite sedition or insurrection against the government of a state; a plot; as a *conspiracy* against the life of a king; a *conspiracy* against the government." Suddenly, we get into something much juicier: crime, treason, sedition, insurrection often aimed at something in government. Interesting. To this day, this is what the majority of conspiracy theories are actually aimed at, yet Webster wrote this 200 years ago!

We will see more of this in a later chapter, but Webster actually adds as his only proof, a conspiracy that forty Jews had plotted against the Apostle Paul to kill him. "When it was day, the Jews made a plot and bound themselves by an oath neither to eat nor drink till they had killed Paul. There were more than forty who made this conspiracy. They went to the chief priests and elders and said, 'We have strictly bound ourselves by an oath to taste no food till we have killed Paul. Now therefore you, along with the council, give notice to the tribune to bring him down to you, as though you were going to determine his case more exactly. And we are ready to kill him before he comes near'" (Acts 23:12-15). It was a different America when a proof for a secular definition came from the Bible. These Jews were the religious leaders, deeply in bed with the political elites of their day, so the text fits his definition. Clearly, conspiracies of high-level politics have been with us for a long, long time.

His second definition is also worth reading. "In law, an agreement between two or more persons, falsely and maliciously to indict, or procure to be indicted, an innocent person of felony." Notice that this is not benign in motivation. It is malicious. It goes after innocent people to protect the guilty. So, it appears that what this first word of the phrase brings to our under-standing is that evil people do malicious, seditious, criminal, and even treasonous things, things they plan in secret which no one knows about but themselves.

Let's turn to the word "theory." This is an interesting word. This time, I will begin with the 1828 definition. Webster calls it, "Speculation, a doctrine or scheme of things, which terminates in speculation or contemplation." He adds that this is "here taken in an unfavorable sense." Meanwhile, the first definition given by the present Webster's is, "A plausible or scientifically acceptable general principle or body of principles offered to explain phenomena."

So here we have a negative and a positive definition for a theory. One means speculation; the other essentially deals with science (to be fair, the 1828 has as the second definition, "An exposition of the general principles of any science; as the *theory* of music"). What I am noticing here is a possible difference in how people can view the phrase "conspiracy theory." Some view it as a scientifically oriented investigation concerning public facts that don't quite add up, perhaps something like the way Sherlock Holmes always went about solving a case.

However, given what we saw with the CIA's covert operation to literally change the phrase and make it something people will not want to engage in, it seems that they wanted people to think of it according to some kind of untethered, wild and crazy speculation, grounded in nothing but the fancies and imaginations of crazy people creating the theory. This is precisely how many people define the phrase today and it is quite troubling, indeed.

When people use the phrase "conspiracy theory" today, it is for the purpose of being a thought stopper and an argument killer. All you have to do these days to make sure no one questions what you are saying is to label those who disagree as conspiracy theorists. Game over. Like a man-made weaponized virus, its sole purpose is to infect a person's mind and destroy all attempts it might make to question an official story. Worse, as one friend told me just today, it is used in a demeaning way, often accompanied with mocking, snide comments. It is ridicule, not reason.

That may not be the spoken or even understood intent of everyone using the term. Nevertheless, it should be without question that this is what the term in fact is used for much of the time. If you throw out "conspiracy theory" towards a person or idea that they are entertaining, you are effectively telling them that they are crazy, kooks, wackos, or worse, enemies of state or the republic itself. That's exactly how the CIA and Bush talked about the phrase. And it is has worked itself out to perfection in the common parlance and understanding of its meaning. This is a massive shift from the way the phrase and the idea behind it was used in days gone by.

CONSPIRACY THEORY AND YOU

How do you understand the phrase? How do you use it? Is it through the CIA's negative propaganda machine or is it more positively—not that the contents of the conspiracy are positive, but that the endeavor itself can be a scientific endeavor? In the latter case, I think the phrase is really just descriptive of someone who disagrees with the mainline story of events. In the former, it demonizes those who disagree with the mainline story of events. That's quite a difference, isn't it?

A BRIEF HISTORY OF CONSPIRACIES

CONFIDENTIAL

REGRADED ~~SECRET~~
Authority NND 750065
By CR/GT, NARS, Date MARCH 15, 1976

SECRET WRITING

EXEMPT from automatic declassification
per. E.O. 11652, Sec. 5(E)(2)
Turner, CIA 28 JAN 1978
Name Agency Date
A 2020
Reason Review on:

A NEW PHENOMENON?

A LOT OF PEOPLE THINK THAT conspiracy theories are a new phenomenon. This is anything but the case. For if that were true, it would mean that there have been no conspiracies in human history. How would I say this? Because, where there are no conspiracies, there is nothing real that causes people to doubt an official narrative. At best, the doubt comes from their own wild imagination. Most things in life are not conspiracies. Most things in life are also not questioned. Granted, most things in life are also relatively unimportant too. But in a conspiracy, any conspiracy, there are always holes in the story.

Those holes are what causes questions to arise. Those questions then lead to doubts and doubts lead to conspiracy theories. But many events in history have led people to doubt an official story. In some of those, we know that not everything happened as the party line told the people. In fact, in some of those, real conspiracies were taking place. In this chapter, I want to give a brief history of a particular form of conspiracy theory known as the false flag. Much of the material for this chapter has been culled from different talks given by Richard Dolan, who has done some tremendous work on this history of conspiracy theories. My work is indebted to him.

WHAT IS A FALSE FLAG?

First, I should ask, what is a false flag? The term comes from the world of pirating on the high seas. Ahoy, Matey! (Did you know you can translate the previous sentence into "Pirate" using Google: *"Th' term comes from th' world o' piratin' on th' high seas."* But I digress). This is the world of Captain Jack Sparrow and the Black Pearl. But this is no Disney movie or theme park ride!

A pirate would sail his ship near to an enemy vessel with the enemy's flag or a neutral flag raised aloft his own, thus fooling them into thinking he was friendly. Then, suddenly, he would raise the skull and crossbones and attack. Why would he do that? First, because pirates really did have a code of honor, unlike those who pull off today's false flag events! Second, the flag itself would terrify the opposition. It reminds me, a Denver Broncos fan, of those horrible days when the Oakland Raiders won for themselves this famous poem from NFL Film's legendary Sam Spence:

The Autumn Wind is a pirate
Blustering in from sea
With a rollicking song he sweeps along
swaggering boisterously

His face is weather beaten
He wears a hooded sash
With his silver hat about his head
And a bristly black moustache
He growls as he storms the country
A villain big and bold
And the trees all shake and quiver and quake
As he robs them of their gold
The Autumn wind is a Raider
Pillaging just for fun
He'll knock you 'round and upside down
And laugh when he's conquered and won.

Only when a cannonball was about to rip through his personal cabin would the poor, unsuspecting captain realize that it was really a pirate who was staring at him across his bow.

We find the language of "false flag" being used as early as the 1680s. One novel of the period tells us,

> But they had hardly shifted sails what way, when they were discovered by the three galleys and a man of war, belonging to the island, which having deceived them with *a false flag*, attacked them so unexpectedly, that the Egyptian captain, being unable to defend himself against so great a force, was obliged to yield up himself, his slaves, ship and all. [spelling modernized, italics mine][13]

The *Elements of International Law* of 1863 gives us a history of how false flags on the high seas were becoming so common, not just among pirates but among nations going off to battle, that international law had to be created to mitigate the problem.

> By the 42d article of the treaty of the 30th of April, 1725, between Spain and Austria, it was agreed that whoever took

---

[13] Sieur de la Roberdiere, *Love Victorious: Or, the Adventures of Oronces and Eugenia. A Novel*, trans. J. E. (London: R. Bentley and S. Magnes, 1684), 117-18.

letters of marque and reprisal from any government not his own should be treated as a pirate, and by the 5th article of the treaty concluded with the Netherlands in 1714, and by the 14th article of the celebrated treaty of 1795 with the United States, it was agreed that whoever took commissions or letters of marque from another State, which was at war with either of the contracting parties, should be considered in the same character of pirates ... The privateer ordinance of Spain of 1801 ... establishes that every vessel shall be considered as a pirate which raises a false flag, or raises no flag, or fights under another flag than its true one.[14]

Breaking these rules was considered "extremely severe." Thus, we find at the outbreak of WWI,

A spectator had asserted that he saw that the attacking German ships which bombarded [Scarborough] had hoisted the British ensign. [This] would, if verified, be a grave breach of international law if the British ensign remained hoisted after the bombardment had begun. At sea, as on land, the use of false colours in war is forbidden.[15]

The language of false flags has in more modern times come to be used of deliberately planned attacks blamed on one party when in fact they were perpetrated by someone else. At their heart, false flags are a form of propaganda. But they move beyond words to actions, actions which often have a fatal outcome for some people.

They are usually done so that other preplanned outcomes, anything from changing public opinion on a matter (opinion that would never change were they not seeing the false flag unfold before their eyes), to passing authoritarian laws, or justifying military invasions, or promulgating some otherwise difficult to

---

[14] Henry Wheaton, *Elements of International Law* (London: Sampson Low, Son & Company, 1863), 255.

[15] "False Flags," *The Law Times*, 138 (Dec 26, 1914), 198; in The Law and the Lawyers, CXXXVIII (London, Windsor House, Nov 1914 - April 1915).

impossible-to-sell-to-the-public outcome. The relations to conspiracy theories is easy to see when you realize that things like mass school shootings, the fall of the twin towers, or the release of deadly diseases into a population are called both conspiracy theories *and* false flags.

PSYOPS

False flags overlap with what the military calls PSYOPs (psychological operations). These are, according to the Department of Defense, "Planned operations to convey selected information and indicators to foreign audiences to influence their emotions, motives, objective reasoning, and ultimately the behavior of ... governments, organizations, groups, and individuals in a manner favorable to the originator's objectives."[16] That's not frightening, is it?

According to our intelligence agencies, there are three forms of these: white, gray, and black. *White PSYOPs* are openly official statements made by the government. Someone in the government tells you something and it becomes the "official" story. It is interesting that they call these "true and factual."[17] Why then are they called PSYOPs? Do not presidents and senators lie from time to time? Does what they lie about not in fact become the official statement of the government? Given those self-evident truths, I'm pretty sure that white-ops engage in more than truth. Many of them engage in white lies and disinformation.

Gray PSYOPs originate in the government, but the source of the information is left deliberately ambiguous to the public. "The activity engaged in plausibly appears to emanate from a non-

---

[16] *Military Information Support Operations: Joint Publication 3-13.2* (Jan 7, 2010), vii, https://jfsc.ndu.edu/Portals/72/Documents/JC2IOS/Additional_Reading/1C1_JP_3-13-2.pdf.

[17] *181. Paper Prepared by the Operations Coordinating Board*, "Foreign Relations of the United States, 1950-11955, The Intelligence Community, 1950-1955," (Washington, May 14, 1954), Heading 2: Definitions. https://history.state.gov/historicaldocuments/frus1950-55Intel/d181.

official American source, or an indigenous, non-hostile source, or there may be no attribution."[18] This is their own language.

So, for example, in a gray PSYOP, the government can use motion pictures to control and influence people to a predetermined outcome. In 1943, several years before the CIA came into existence, the Office of Strategic Services created an 11-page memo titled, "The Motion Picture as a Weapon of Psychological Warfare." We found out about this memo in 2004 when it was declassified. Its objective is, "To exploit the potentialities of the motion picture as a weapon of psychological warfare for the United States." It says motion pictures can and have been employed as PSYOPs against "the civilians and the armed forces of the United States," her "allies," "prisoners of war or antagonistic groups in neutral countries," or "the peoples of enemy and enemy occupied countries." They explicitly say they will and have used propaganda through short-wave broadcasting stations and many of the Hollywood companies of the day. And this was in 1943![19]

Another example is the news information in a newspaper or on television that poses as objective journalism, when the truth is it is anything but that. The infamous Project Mockingbird, which should be required reading for all grade-schoolers in my opinion, is another classic example of a known gray PSYOP.

This secret operation "officially" ran from March – June of 1963, involved wiretapping of a handful of journalists,[20] but was part of a larger clandestine and highly coordinated CIA disinformation campaign that ran from the 1940s through 1970s.[21] This

---

[18] Ibid.

[19] You can find the memo at, "The Motion Picture As A Weapon of Psychological Warfare," *Speak Project* (Apr 13, 2020), https://projectspeak.net/the-motion-picture-as-a-weapon-of-psychological-warfare.

[20] This is revealed in the declassified CIA report called "Family Jewels" (1973), which can be accessed on the CIAs website as part of the Freedom of Information Act.

[21] The unveiling of Mockingbird and the larger CIA coverup to the world was Carl Bernstein's "The CIA and the Media: How America's Most Powerful News Media Worked Hand in Glove with the Central Intelligence Agency and Why the Church Committee Covered It Up," *Rolling Stone* (Oct 20, 1977): 55-67. During

involved not less than 400 high ranking journalists from the likes of *Time, The New York Times, The Washington Post, CBS, ABC, NBC, Reuters, United Press International (UPI), Associated Press (AP)*, you name it, all receiving paychecks from the CIA! Of course, none of this was known *at the time.*

Many of these journalists were simply committing subterfuge against the Evil Empire (as Reagan would later call the Soviet Union) during the cold war and thought of their own actions as highly patriotic. Many of them probably were. But not all of them. There were also gray-ops being committed against the people of the United States. This is all known, well-established fact of history now, despite Wikipedia's astroturfing (see the last chapter of this book for a definition) that "Operation Mockingbird is an alleged large-scale program..." Mockingbird might be alleged as "large-scale," but whatever we want to call the larger operation, it is simply a matter of public historical record.

Does this continue today? Many people don't even know that it happened in the past, so of course most people think it doesn't happen today. But consider the following. First, ponder the likes of John Brennan, Michael Hayden, James Clapper, Juan Zarate, Anderson Cooper, and Jack Keane.[22] Brennan is the former director of the CIA and is a senior national security and intelligence analyst for MSNBC. Hayden is the former Director of the NSA and works for CNN. Clapper is the former US Director of National Intelligence who now works for CNN. Zarate was Deputy National Security Advisor to President Bush (W.) and works for CBS. Cooper is a Vanderbilt (i.e. one of the wealthiest families in America) who spent two terms in the CIA as an intern and now

---

the Church Committee, the Chairman asked, "Do you have any people being paid by the CIA who are contributing to the national news services, AP and UPI?" The answer? "Well again I think we are running into the kind of detail, Mr. Chairman, that I would prefer to handle in executive session."

[22] This list comes from a *YouTube* presentation Dolan and his wife did. See Richard Dolan, "Media Control & Mockingbird Today," *Youtube* (April 16, 2019), https://www.youtube.com/watch?v=EIA7sl827iQ.

works for CNN. Keane is a four-star general and works as a neo-con analyst for Fox News. No conflict of interest in any of this, right? How in the world do Americans think people who used to work at the highest levels of our national intelligence make for unbiased journalistic reporting? Answer? They have no idea who these people are. But this is a very old CIA tactic. As Bernstein reported,

> The CIA even ran a formal training program in the 1950s to teach its agents to be journalists. Intelligence officers were 'taught to make noises like reporters,' explained a high CIA official, and were then placed in major news organiza-tions with help from management.[23]

Second, consider statements like the one made from Mika Brzezinski, a political commentator for MSNBC who is the daugh-ter of Zbigniew Brzezinski—organizer of the Trilateral Commis-sion, counselor to Lyndon Johnson and Jimmy Carter, and a man deeply involved in overseeing propaganda throughout the world.[24] Mika rather notoriously said that Donald Trump is trying to un-dermine media by making up his own facts thereby controlling what people actually think. "And that's our job."[25]

Similarly, Amber Lyon, 3x Emmy Award-Winning Journalist told us that governments like Bahrain (and our own!) were paying CNN to present their countries in a positive light and to even make up false stories. She actually said that CNN makes up fake news for the state.[26] Then there is one of the leading German journalists, the

---

[23] Bernstein, 57.

[24] For example, Matt Mulhern, "Excellent Propaganda" Zbigniew Brzezinski's Narrative for the Soviet Invasion of Afghanistan, MA Thesis to CUNY City College (2019).

[25] Mika Brzezinski, MSNBC Morning Joe, *MSNBC* (Feb 22, 2017).

[26] Glenn Greenwald, "CNN and the Business of State-Sponsored TV News," The Guardian (Sept 4, 2012),
https://www.theguardian.com/commentisfree/2012/sep/04/cnn-business-state-sponsored-news.

now deceased Udo Ulfkotte who maintained that journalists like himself and leading newspapers were publishing material that was being fed to them, or bought, by the CIA and other Western intelligence agencies.[27] Of course, you won't find this information on mainstream news sites, *unless they are calling it a conspiracy*! But this leads to one of the great ironies of our age that these media conglomerates, in bed with the American intelligence agencies for over 60 years are now telling us that they are our Big Brother protectors saving us from all the world's "fake news."

Here we need to stop for just a moment and consider just why it is that the news these days is so confusing to people. Is it really just as simple as saying that one side is biased and the other is unbiased (that's laughably absurd), or even as saying that one side is "conservative" and the other is "liberal?" We know for a fact that the CIA and others have infiltrated our own media in order to commit gray PSYOPs on its own people, and it sure seems like that hasn't stopped to this day. William Casey, another former director of the CIA once said, "We'll know our disinformation program is complete when everything the US public believes is false."[28] But just remember, this is really a very old idea. Thomas Jefferson long ago said, "Nothing can now be believed which is seen in a newspaper. Truth itself becomes suspicious by being put into that polluted vehicle ... I will add, that the man who never looks into a newspaper is better informed than he who reads them."[29]

---

[27] "Controversial Publicist Udo Ulfkotte is Dead," Spiegel Culture (Jan 14, 2017), https://www.spiegel.de/kultur/literatur/udo-ulfkotte-umstrittener-publizist-und-ehemaliger-faz-journalist-ist-tot-a-1130008.html.

[28] William J. Casey, first staff meeting, 1981. The source of the quote comes from Barbara Honegger (former assistant to the chief domestic policy adviser to President Reagan) who told it to Senior White House correspondent Sarah McClendon, who made it public. See the excellent work done tracking this down by Melissa Melton, *The War on Liberty*, https://thewaronliberty.com/william-casey-well-know-our-disinformation-program-is-complete-when-everything-the-american-public-believes-is-false/.

[29] *Letter from Thomas Jefferson to John Norvell, Date: June 11, 1807, Page 2 of 3*, Source Collection: The Thomas Jefferson Papers at the Library of Congress, Series 1:

There is an amazing compilation video you can watch on *YouTube* that sets 36 different local newscasts side by side. They all say the exact same thing. Word for word. Though this happens almost nightly, listen to the content of one special unbiased, unique piece of journalistic sleuthing. It's stunning:

> Our greatest responsibility is to serve our (FILL IN THE BLANK) communities. We are extremely proud of the quality, balanced journalism that (LOCAL CHANNEL) produces. But, we are concerned about the troubling trend of irresponsible, one-sided news stories plaguing our county. The sharing of biased and false news has become all too common on social media. More alarming, some media outlets publish these same fake stories, without checking facts first. Unfortunately, some members of national media outlets are using their platforms to push their own personal bias and agenda to control exactly what people think. This is extremely dangerous to our democracy.[30]

They literally say this with a straight faced, and no, I'm not talking about the fact that we are not a democracy, but a democratic republic. I'm talking about how scores and scores of stations are all saying word-for-word the exact same thing about how people fake the news and don't do their homework. Hmmm. Maybe these poor talking-heads didn't do theirs either?

If this is true, then the news is deliberately confusing by the very people who make it, especially when someone else comes

---

General Correspondence. 1651-1827, Microfilm Reel: 038, https://www.loc.gov/resource/mtj1.038_0592_0594/?sp=2&st=text. It's interesting, I found this quotation looking up the origin one said to be from Mark Twain, "If you don't read the newspaper you are uninformed. If you do read the newspaper you are misinformed." This Twain quotation is, ironically enough, fodder for its own small conspiracy theory. Fact is, he never said it.

[30] There are several places you can find this montage. Here is one. "Scripted Local News Compilation – All Spouting the Same Garbage," *YouTube* (Apr 8, 2018), https://www.youtube.com/watch?time_continue=515&v=wF0VGnmLExc&feature=emb_logo.

along and challenges them on their truthfulness. This creates and fosters a need for conspiracy theories simply so people can try to make sense of that which is itself nonsensical but is being portrayed as the official narrative. All this does is make the whole thing grow like an out of control monster. But this Godzilla is not going to come and save anyone.

The third form of PSYOP is *a black-op*. These are "partially or completely fabricated [events] ... made to appear credible to the target audience."[31] These definitely do not let you know that the government is behind it. They "appear to emanate from a source ... usually hostile in nature." And that is the definition of a false flag.

A BRIEF HISTORY OF KNOWN FALSE FLAGS

In the following pages, I will give a brief history of known false flags (which of course were not known at the time) as outlined and discussed in the excellent TV series *False Flags* by Richard Dolan.[32] Much of the descriptions are his, though I have put them into my own words. I won't give you all of his list of false flags, in hopes that you might go and see his program for yourself. It is both fascinating and well made. The purpose of this is to demonstrate that real conspiracies, in this case through covert operations of high-ranking order, have, do, and will continue to happen. We know about them. They are not a secret. The real story has been made known by historians, through declassification of vital government documents, or other means.

The Burning of Rome

On July 18, 64 AD, a fire began in Rome which raged for more than five days. It ended up destroying between a third to

---

[31] *Paper Prepared by the Operations Coordinating Board*, Heading 2.
[32] Richard Dolan, *False Flags*, 1 Season, 10 Episodes, *Gaia* (2017).

two thirds of the eternal city. What happened? Though we do not have any original sources, and really only one secondary source, it appears that the fire was set, deliberately, by Nero.

It turns out that Nero wanted to build a series of palaces called Domus Aurea ("Golden House") that would have taken a huge amount of space, space not available in Rome at the time. Nero tried to get the senate to agree to tear down many structures to build his dream, but they refused. Suddenly, the great fire took down those very structures and almost all the land he needed was available. Because of this, rumors quickly spread that Nero started the fire.

Now, according to the historian Tacitus, Nero was 30 miles from Rome in the city of Antium when the fire broke out. Furthermore, parts of Nero's own palace were caught up in the blaze, and Nero apparently rushed back to Rome to help put the fire out, along with helping the newly homeless who were in need of food and supplies. Thus, many think from this that Nero had nothing to do with the fire.

But this is hardly proof of anything. Facts are that Nero ended up giving himself most of the newly emptied land so that he could in fact build his palace. Furthermore, there is no need for Nero to be in Rome when the fires began. Lackeys could easily set blazes while he fiddled by the sea.

Because he could not squelch the persistent rumors, Nero found himself a scapegoat—the Christians. These are the people the letter of Romans was written to, probably even many of the names we find in its last chapter. Christians were meeting in secret (no thanks to him and his predecessors' continual persecutions against them!), would not worship Caesar, were said to be cannibals (eating the body and blood of their god), and were anticipating the end of the world and the demise of Rome. They were viewed akin to terrorists by many proper citizens. They made for perfect patsies. As a repercussion for their outrageous attempt to destroy the Empire by lighting Rome on fire, Nero began having Christians fed to lions in the Coliseum. Is there any wonder so many Christians believed that he was The Antichrist whose mark was 666?

Was this a false flag? We honestly do not know. It has many key features (which I will discuss in the last chapter), and this is the important thing. It was a spectacular and emotional event. The news spread quickly of treachery by the Emperor. A scapegoat was quickly found by the man in power. He then commits decisive and negative action against that scapegoat.

But it lacks the most important thing: evidence. Granted, it was nearly 2,000 years ago. The point here, however, is that even if it wasn't a false flag, there is no question but that two divergent conspiracy theories vied for power. Who caused the fire? Nero? The Christians? Almost no one said it was just an accident. This was not mere watercooler gossip fodder. People's lives were on the line. In the end, he who had the physical power got to write the story. Christians were murdered. And in the eyes of many, they were the conspirators who tried to destroy the Empire.

The Inquisition

For 200 years, from the 1250s to the mid 1400s, the Holy Inquisition was established by the Roman Church to combat heresy. This itself could be the subject of several conspiracy theories, as how many people did they blame for wrongdoing and believing when in fact they were doing no such thing? How much wealth did it acquire for itself through the Inquisition? However, Dolan focuses on just one aspect of it. In 1487, the *Malleus Maleficarum* ("The Hammer of Witches") was published. It was essentially the ancient version of the Monte Python Holy Grail scene, "Burn her, She's a Witch" put to writing, but hopefully with a bit more logic than the skit. It became the source of much human suffering through the obvious scare tactics made famous in America in the Salem Witch Trials.

The idea was, you incite increasing hatred of witches in the public, you begin to terrify them about witches and how they mean to destroy you and your eternal soul. Then you run to the rescue by rounding them all up and killing them, or rather, by bringing them to the church who would then give them a very "fair" trial ... and then kill them.

But of course, there was more to it than this. The whole practice of indulgences, which made Martin Luther so furious, was used. If you or your family member was a witch, you could pay the church to reduce the sentence—either in this life or in the life to come. Furthermore, the Church lined its pockets by seizing the lands of witches, which made for obvious false flag opportunities, when you consider that they were always wanting more land. How do you get the land? Say that the owners were witches. Estimations are that over 1,000,000 European women were put to death as witches as a result of the Inquisition.

Gunpowder Plot

On November 5, 1605, Robert Catesby and a group of his Roman Catholic friends plotted to kill King James I and blow up Parliament in an attempt to replace the Protestant leadership with Catholic leadership. However, on November 4, one of the conspirators, Guy Fawkes, was discovered in the cellar of the House of Lords with many barrels of gunpowder in his possession. Eventually, he and the others were tried and executed for treason. For this reason, to this day, every November 5, the British celebrate Guy Fawkes Day by burning Fawkes in effigy. The question is, how was Fawkes discovered?

The story goes that an anonymous letter was sent to the authorities, warning of them of the conspiracy. The king's soldiers were sent to Parliament to search, and lo and behold, they found Fawkes. For saving Parliament and the king and queen, the whole ordeal was spun as the salvation of Britain. It quickly became a national holiday.

But there are strange out-of-place facts to the official narrative. First, Fawkes was not found in a basement room but was rather on a ground floor room which was easily rented. The official story was wrong. The letter, while of unknown origin, made its way into the hands of Robert Cecil, the Royal Chancellor and 1st Earl of Salisbury. Cecil was a scheming politician and leader of the War Party, which wanted a war with Spain from which he thought he could profit greatly. He was constantly running spies in the Catholic community of Britain and had his pulse on any and all information worth caring about. Cecil told the king nothing about the plot, save giving him the anonymous letter. Hmmm.

Furthermore, the gunpowder found on the scene was not the kind you would expect to find if people were planning on blowing up Parliament. It was cheap-grade, low quality gun powder. Finally, a Jesuit historian named John Gerard, gave a very different interpretation, which came to light 300 years after the fact, because his testimony was suppressed. "When we examine into the details supplied to us as to the progress of the affair, we find that much of what the conspirators are said to have done is well-nigh incredible, while it is utterly impossible that if they really acted in the manner described, the public authorities should not have had full knowledge of their proceedings."[33] It seems a strong possibility that Cecil (and presumably others) either staged the plot or knew about it ahead of time and didn't tell anyone; they just let it play into their hands, for out of this, Catholic persecution intensified and hopes were high that England would resume its war with Spain.

Russian Cossack False Flag

King Gustav III of Sweden was an unpopular despot. He had seized power in a coup d'état against the parliament, in an

---

[33] John Gerard, *What Was the Gunpowder Plot? The Traditional Story Tested by Original Evidence* (Osgood, McIlvane, 1897).

attempt to re-create an absolute monarchy. It didn't entirely work; the Riksdag of the Estates was wounded, but not killed. Nobody liked him, including the nobility. Russia openly supported his political opponents and so Gustav believed war was only a matter of time. He very much wanted a war, but he still needed parliament to declare it. He was alone. No one else in Sweden wanted war. So, Gustav tried to provoke one instead.

In June 1788, a Swedish fleet met a Russian counterpart in the Baltic Sea, but the Russian commander would not engage, and the Swedes went away without their war. Enter Gustav's false flag. A head tailor of the Royal Swedish Opera received an order to sew a bunch of Russian Cossack uniforms. The Swedish army then staged an attack on June 27, 1788 on its own outpost in the middle of nowhere in a place called Puumala. A state fighting against itself, killing its own people, just to get the outcome it wanted? Couldn't be, right?

Many of the king's critics discovered the ruse and declared the king's war illegal. But it didn't matter, because the populace had already been whipped up into a foaming frenzy by the media of its day, controlled, of course, by the crown itself. This in turn put pressure on Parliament which called for a "defensive" war on Russia. The false flag worked, and Sweden got its war with Russia. Unfortunately for the Swedes, the Russians kicked their little tails. 22,000 Swedish soldiers were killed, the war lasted only three years, the Fins concocted their own false flag and gained independence from Sweden, and the king was assassinated in 1792.

Sinking of the USS Maine

On Feb 15th, 1898, the USS Maine sank in the Havana Harbor. Its sinking lead directly to the outbreak of the Spanish-American War later that April. Commissioned just three years earlier, the Maine was an armored cruiser of the U.S. Navy. Because of its 9-year protracted construction, she was virtually obsolete at the time of completion.

The Maine was sent to the Havana Harbor in Cuban water by President McKinley to protect U.S. interests during the Cuban War of Independence. After only a month, she blew up and sank in the harbor, killing three-quarters of her crew. A U.S. Navy board of inquiry called the Sampson Board insisted that the ship had been sunk by an external explosion from a mine, in other words, sabotage. Some Navy officers disagreed, arguing that the ship's magazines had been ignited by a spontaneous fire in a coal bunker inside the boat. Neither group pointed guilt at anyone specifically.

William Randolph Hearst, millionaire builder of the beautiful Hearst Castle and then owner of the *New York Journal*, and Joseph Pulitzer, the famous namesake of the Pulitzer Prizes which he established and owner of the *New York World*, provided intense coverage of the sinking. Their "yellow journalism" tabloids exaggerated and distorted whatever information they could find, sometimes even lying, making up news when none of the facts fit their agenda. Hearst soon was offering a reward of $50,000 for the conviction of the criminals who sent 258 American sailors to their deaths. Both were promoting a war with Spain. Why? No one knows for sure. But with popular slogans like, "Remember the Maine, to hell with Spain," they incited the American populace to virtually beg for war. They got it along with a lot of spoils. As for Spain, she conducted her own investigation and found that the sinking was an accident, but it was too late.

Over the years, different inquiries into the sinking have been undertaken. In 1911, a study concluded that it was likely a mine that caused the ship to capsize. In the 1970s, options were swayed in the opposite direction by a new study. In 1995, the Smithsonian turned opinions back to the sabotage theory. They had uncovered evidence from "an unimpeachable witness," Alexander Bryce, an American diplomat who had given testimony in 1911 but was ignored. He was in Cuba and had many informants working for him. One of these was a former Spanish officer who told him days before the explosion that the fanatic officers loyal to the brutal governor General Valeriano Weyler were planning to sink the Maine.

While there has never been any evidence that the Americans did it to themselves, this story is important because it gives lessons that would later be incorporated into modern false flags. The media could whip people up to turn opinion almost overnight, especially through shocking events that make them mad. State goals dovetailed with media propaganda. There was an immediate identification of a culprit and a call for violent action. And so on.

Pearl Harbor

Dolan gives many more examples, some of which are still relevant today. These include false flags committed by the United States to get us into WWI, some spectacular false flags by the Nazis, Soviets, and Chinese to bring about war in their own countries, false flags during the Cold War, and on into the 21st century. But since I want you to watch his show and I do not want to lose my overall focus by entering into too deep of water, I'll only give one more. This one will probably surprise many readers. It is the attack on Pearl Harbor.

It was truly a day that will live forever in infamy: December 7, 1941. The location is Honolulu, in the then U.S. Territory of Hawaii. It was just before 8:00am on a Sunday. Suddenly, out of nowhere, the Imperial Japanese Navy committed a surprise, preemptive strike against the United States. Much of our Pacific fleet was destroyed and I've actually been to the U.S.S. Arizona and the Pearl Harbor National Memorial and seen it for myself. The results immediately changed public opinion about World War II. Prior to this, Americans were decisively against entering the war on either front. It took only a single day for Congress to declare war on Japan and by the end of the week, we were surrounded by war, having entered the European side of it by Dec 11.

So where's the false flag? Most people are under the assumption that the reason the Japanese were able to hit us is because our military intelligence simply failed. Everyone from the President on down to ma and pa running the local General Store were in the dark. But even at the time, there were some who thought that Pearl Harbor was a setup.

In recent times, meticulous evidence has arisen from government sources through the Freedom of Information Act that demonstrate beyond the shadow of doubt that President Roosevelt knew about the Japanese plans more than a year in advance.[34] The main files, called the Pacific War Communications Intelligence (PWCINT) files, contained over a million records of events surrounding WWII. Enough information came out of these files that we know for certain that the military high command knew about the specific attacks more than a week in advance. How did they know? Military intelligence had cracked the Japanese codes more than a year earlier, by October of 1940. They knew almost everything the Japanese were doing! The whole idea that we didn't know an attack was coming, what it was coming, that the Japanese were in total radio silence that day … it was all false. All of our knowledge was sent on to the headquarters for Navy Intelligence in Washington D.C.

The problem was, though we could have defended ourselves, the key information was withheld from the commanders in Hawaii. Lt. General Walter Short and Admiral Husband E. Kimmel did not know anything about the eminent attack. Both lived, but more than 2,000 of our own military officers did not.

What's so interesting about this event is not that somehow the U.S. was really behind Pearl Harbor. Of course, it was the

---

[34] See Robert B. Stinnett, *Day of Deceit: The Truth about FDR and Pearl Harbor* (New York: The Free Press, 2000).

Japanese. This was not some covert operation of the United States against its own people. Instead, it was—much as we saw suggested with the gunpowder plot, the United States doing nothing to prevent an attack that they could have stopped easily had they wished. Why would they do it? Because the leading heads of state in the government desperately wanted to get involved in WWII but the American people did not. It took Pearl Harbor to change their minds. And what an immediate job it did of that.

Don't get me wrong. If any war in the last 1000 years was justifiable to enter, it was WWII. The atrocities going on all over the planet were of such horrendous magnitude that they had to be stopped. It was not a bad thing for America to enter WWII. But to do it at the cost of your own people? To do it while lying to your own people, making them think one thing when the opposite was true? That's classic black PSYOPs kind of subterfuge.

The purpose of this chapter has been to help you see that conspiracies have been going on a long, long time. Furthermore, when conspiracies arise, doubts and questions also arise. Out of them come conspiracy theories. Because certain people pressed long and hard enough, eventually, those conspiracies were brought to light and the conspiracy theory was no longer a theory, but fact. This is the importance of engaging in alternative views of questionable events. But I'm guessing that many Christians, even still, while perhaps even having a hard time swallowing some of the material in this chapter, still need more help thinking through the dark world of conspiracies and conspiracy theories. So, the next chapter will turn to biblical thinking about these questions.

A BRIEF BIBLICAL THEOLOGY OF CONSPIRACIES

CONSPIRACIES IN THE BIBLE

IT'S ONE THING TO TALK ABOUT false flags and government PSYOPs. This is the realm of the secular world around us, after all. Some Christians probably think a "good Christian" should not even worry about such worldly things as these. I would strongly argue otherwise, as Jesus has left us to live in this world and being naïve about what goes on here does not help us be proper salt and light, speak the truth, or be wise as serpents and innocent as doves in the places we live.

It is another thing to move this to the realm of Holy Scripture. I'm pretty sure I have never seen someone attempt a biblical theology of conspiracies before. Perhaps the main reason I wanted to write this book was to help Christians think through what I believe is a very significant issue facing all of us in the 21st century. I believe that looking into what the Bible says about conspiracies can be helpful to that end. Thus, I offer up my own short history of conspiracies in the Bible. I think you might just find yourself being surprised at how many and how important to biblical history these conspiracies and the theories that spawned them actually are.

Joseph and his Brothers

The first time I can find the word "conspiracy" in an English Bible is Genesis 37. This is the story of Joseph, that spoiled favorite son of Jacob whom his older brothers all came to despise. Vs. 18 says, "They saw him from afar, and before he came near to them they *conspired* against him to kill him." The conspiracy was between the ten older brothers. It was a secret pact between them. They did not let their father in on the plot. Francis Schaeffer tells us the moral problem:

> As far as the moral situation is concerned, although the total external result has yet to come, the reality of it is already upon them. "They conspired against him to slay him...." "Come now therefore, and let us slay him, and cast him into some pit, and we will say, Some evil beast hath devoured him: and we shall see what will become of his dreams." They are perfectly willing to kill their brother and break their father's heart. All these things arose in the internal world of their thoughts, in their hatred, in their envy, not in the external world. The sin of the brothers was not when they sold Joseph to Egypt, but in the reality of the internal world. It is the internal world of thought that distinguishes man as man … [they broke] the commandment not to covet.[35]

---

[35] Francis A. Schaeffer, *The Complete Works of Francis A. Schaeffer: A Christian Worldview*, vol. 3 (Westchester, IL: Crossway Books, 1982), 303–304.

It is vital to see that conspiracies begin internally, not externally and that they are hidden in secret until the plot is carried out, where even then, the true actions are blurred from all public sight. This is called sin and it is a major factor behind conspiracies. It is also a vital doctrine that we will come back to in the last chapter.

Of course, the story plays itself out. Joseph did not in fact die, and since he knew what they had done to him, once he came to power in Egypt, he was able, in God's timing, to let the conspiracy be known to everyone. The most important theological point this whole sordid story makes comes at the very end of Genesis. Joseph, speaking to his brothers, consoles them with the following words. "As for you, you meant evil against me, but God meant it for good, to bring it about that many people should be kept alive, as they are today" (Gen 50:20). The doctrine is God's absolute sovereignty over the conspiracy. It didn't catch him by surprise. In fact, he had his own good outcome that he wanted to have happen through the wicked actions of Joseph's brothers.

But consider this as a last thought about this conspiracy. Let's say for fun that Benjamin, who was Joseph's younger brother and who had not known about the conspiracy, had gotten wind that Joseph was alive and went to tell his father? Let's say that he had even heard that his brothers were the ones responsible for his disappearance and for lying to Jacob, who now believed the actual conspiracy theory told to them by his sons. How would Benjamin's story have been viewed at the time? It certainly would have been viewed as a conspiracy theory rather than truth, because the truth of the matter had not yet been exposed. This serves to help you see that conspiracy theories can in fact be true, but also helps you understand how it is that they are viewed prior to being made known.

Satan in the Garden

Though the word "conspiracy" is not found prior to this, I would argue that the first conspiracy in Scripture comes in

Genesis 3 at the hands of the devil. The famous Reformer Wilhelmus à Brakel writes, "The devil conspired to cause Adam and Eve to fall in order to prevent them from glorifying God, whom he hated with a dreadful hatred."[36]

The conspiracy here was to lie and then, in the next chapter, to murder. Jesus tells us of both in the same breath as he is undergoing his own personal treatment of being conspired against, as we will look at shortly. "You are of your father the devil, and your will is to do your father's desires. He was a murderer from the beginning, and does not stand in the truth, because there is no truth in him. When he lies, he speaks out of his own character, for he is a liar and the father of lies" (John 8:44). Lies and murder are at the heart of many conspiracies.

It is critical to point out here something in the context that Brakel does not mention. This is the promised Seed that will be given to Eve. The promise is, "I will put enmity between you and the woman, and between your seed and her seed; he shall bruise your head, and you shall bruise his heel" (Gen 3:15). The promise does not come prior to the temptation and fall, but after, meaning that something else was certainly in Satan's mind when he originally tempted our parents.[37] But it surely must play a part in Satan's inciting Cain to murder his brother Abel, who became the first martyr and whose blood is a type of Christ's himself (Heb 12:24). This began the war of the seeds that I write about in my book on biblical Giants. Satan is fighting against the seed of the woman, one who is a type of Christ. He did not want her to have a child that would end up bringing about his own demise.

---

[36] Wilhelmus à Brakel, *The Christian's Reasonable Service*, ed. Joel R. Beeke, trans. Bartel Elshout, vol. 1 (Grand Rapids, MI: Reformation Heritage Books, 1992), 370.
[37] I believe Satan's lie in Genesis 3 was due to the fact that God gave Adam dominion over the earth and, as Psalm 8 hints at, though made "a little lower" than the heavenly beings like Satan, would be the one the devil was supposed to bow down to. In other words, Satan did not want to be under the authority of a ball of mud. The murder of Abel, however, was due more specifically to the seed prophecy.

In this story, we also have to realize that God's prophecy of the seed-war means that he knew Satan would do this and that God had actually planned out the war in advance. This is identical to what we saw with Joseph's brothers and the good purpose that the LORD had in ordaining their treachery. In the Adam and Eve story, God's end-game is to glorify the God-man Jesus Christ who will crush the head of the serpent. And so his sovereignty and omniscience become major factors in the conspiracies found in the Bible. We are told about them so that we might come to trust the God who is sovereign over such secretive and treacherous conspiracies.

Fall of the Angels

There is a second conspiracy prior to Joseph that I want to mention. Though it is not easily discernable from the biblical text, it is crystal clear once you read the oral traditions of the Jews which the NT Christians like Jude and Peter took quite seriously. This concerns the fall of the angels.

In the fuller Brakel quotation above, he takes the very common view that the angels had sinned "and become devils" prior to Satan's conspiracy in the Garden. There may actually be a hint or two in the Scripture that there were other fallen heavenly beings there with Adam and Eve and that Satan's conspiracy went deeper than just his own private envy and hatred.

Ezekiel, using supernaturally charged mythical imagery of the Garden of Eden talks about "stones of fire." He says, "You were an anointed guardian cherub. I placed you; you were on the holy mountain of God; in the midst of the stones of fire you walked" (Ezek 28:14). Gregory the Great (c. 540–604) gives a typical commentary on this, "He gave the names of nine stones, since there are nine ranks of angels. The first angel was adorned and covered with these nine since when it was set ahead of the whole multitude of angels, it was more illustrious in comparison with them."[38] Gregory sees these stones as angelic entities.

Ezekiel 28 has a parallel chapter. This is chapter 31. In both chapters, an earthly king is in mind, but that earthly king has a heavenly counterpart who rules over him in heavenly places. The function of the mythological language is to connect the heavenly and earthly kings as one. In Ch. 31, the stones of fire become "the trees of Eden." "Whom are you thus like in glory and in greatness among the trees of Eden? You shall be brought down with the trees of Eden to the world below" (Ezek 31:18). God does not punish trees; he punishes moral creatures—humans and angels. Given this parallel, it is curious that we are told, "The man and his wife hid themselves from the presence of the LORD God among the trees of the garden" (Gen 3:8). If it is possible that one heavenly being is present here, why not others?[39]

At any rate, when we come to Genesis 6, we learn about a second fall, if you will. This is where the "sons of God" marry the "daughters of man" (literally, daughters of Adam). Taking my view that I exhaustively worked out in the introduction to *Giants: Sons of Gods*, we are dealing here with heavenly beings who fall in their lust for women. This is detailed for us in the book of Enoch, which Jude quotes and alludes to positively over a dozen times in his short letter. The relevant portion reads,

> And the angels, the sons of heaven, saw them and lusted after them, and said to one another: "Come! Let us choose for ourselves wives from people, and we will beget for ourselves children." And Semjâzâ, who was their ruler, said to them: "I fear that you will not desire to do this deed, and I

---

[38] Gregory the Great, "Forty Gospel Homilies 34," cited in Kenneth Stevenson and Michael Gluerup, *Ezekiel, Daniel,* Ancient Christian Commentary on Scripture OT 13 (Downers Grove, IL: InterVarsity Press, 2008), 95.

[39] The explanation for all this cannot be surveyed here, but it deals with Eden as the meeting place of heaven and earth, what is sometimes called a cosmic mountain or the divine council.

alone will be a debtor of a great sin." Therefore they all answered him: "Let us *swear an oath* and let us all *anathematize one another*, not to turn away from *this plan*, until we should complete it and do this deed." Then they all swore together and anathematized one another by it. And these were the two hundred who descend in the days of Jared to the summit of Mount Hermon, and they called the mountain Hermon, because they swore and anathematized one another by it.

(1 En 6:2-6)

This is a conspiracy. *The Expositor's Greek Testament* explains,

> Two hundred of the angels, or watchers, *Egregori* as they are called in the Greek versions of Dan. 4:13 by Aquila and Symmachus, conspired together under the leadership of Semjaza (elsewhere called Azazel) ... Complaint having been made of the sin and misery thus introduced into the world, Raphael is sent down from heaven to bind Azazel hand and foot and shut him up in darkness till the judgment day, when he will be cast into eternal fire.[40]

Again, we see that the conspiracy is at first a secret, but at some point, it becomes known to others. In this case, it is only when God Most High gives the judgment and loyal angels like Raphael are sent to carry out the sentence that the conspiracy becomes known to one and all.

More importantly, we learn from this and the previous story that heavenly beings can be, and apparently often are, involved in conspiracies on the earth. These often include interactions with mankind, as we will see again when we come to the New Testament. Until then, it is enough to say that perhaps this adds a layer of explanation to why some conspiracies are so deeply and powerfully internally rational and logically coherent, whether or

---

[40] J.B. Mayor, "The General Epistle of Jude," in *The Expositor's Greek Testament: Commentary*, vol. 5 (New York: George H. Doran Company, n.d.), 239–240.

not they conform to reality. There are ancient dark intelligences at work in some of them. If one understands this but does not understand that God is greater still, this is the kind of thought that could make a person come undone.

King Saul

King Saul is a fascinating case-study in conspiracy *theories*. This is the king, you must remember, who was chosen by God, anointed by Samuel, but would not be from the eventual lineage of the Messiah. Saul was a conflicted man in almost everything that he did. His life was an increasingly twisted tangled web of conspiracy theories. This especially concerns his harpist, the man who would replace him as king, David. David's succession as king is important, because it grounds all of Saul's conspiracy theories towards him. Those theories were rooted in a truth: David was going to be king and Saul could not stop it.

Rather than get carried away and go through the many cycles of Saul taking David to his side only to cast him away and then blame him for something, perhaps it is best to just look at one particular story: 1 Samuel 22.

David has been on the run from Saul for a couple of chapters. In the meantime, David has been gathering together people who will follow him rather than Saul. A war-ditty was circulating about he and Saul, "Saul has struck down his thousands, and David his ten thousands." All this is interesting, for on the one hand he has been anointed by Samuel already (1Sa 16:13) and Saul obviously knew this, not to mention the fame he was incurring to himself. On the other, Saul was the king and David simply was not trying to overthrow his monarchy. Further, David is only away from Saul's court because Saul was himself trying to kill him! That means, whatever following David gained while on the run would not have occurred had Saul not first forced him to flee. Those are some of the facts that go into trying to understand Saul's twisted mind.

In 1 Samuel 22, David was fleeing some other enemies (the king of Gath). He came to the cave of Adullam and apparently stayed there so long that his entire family heard about it. It was here that he truly began to be recognized as Israel's true leader. Hundreds were coming to him, people in distress as well as fighting men.

He then leaves the cave and went out of Israel's territory to Moab where he befriended the king there. Perhaps Saul perceived this as some kind of threat to his kingship? Perhaps David was planning a war? But the prophet Gad came to David and told him not to remain there, but to head back to Judah. David heeded the words and went to the forest of Hereth. Saul got wind that David was here and the picture from vs. 6 is one of a commander getting ready to fight someone. It says, "Saul was sitting at Gibeah under the tamarisk tree on the height with his spear in his hand, and all his servants were standing about him."

Saul begins to speak to them, knowing that many of them are thinking of joining sides with David. "Hear now, people of Benjamin; will the son of Jesse [David] give every one of you fields and vineyards, will he make you all commanders of thousands and commanders of hundreds, that all of you have conspired against me? Not one discloses to me when my son makes a covenant with the son of Jesse. None of you is sorry for me or discloses to me that my son has stirred up my servant against me, to lie in wait, as at this day." (7-8).

Hear the paranoia in Saul's words. It is paranoia laced with traces of truth. No one did tell them about Jonathan's covenant with David that caused David to flee in the first place ... from Saul's wrath. But did they even know? The earlier story gives no indication that they did. From what we are told, this is Saul's imagination at work, though it is certainly possible that someone did know, which is all part of what makes conspiracy theories so interesting.

As for the second part of his conspiracy theory, every time we read about David in a situation like this, the text is clear that he is not trying to kill Saul or subvert his rule. As for Jonathan, we have a hint that he might have been (he was very angry with his father for humiliating him when David had fled; 20:34), and yet from the character of that man, it is hard to believe. All this makes for more intrigue, though it also points us to the fact that Saul is in fact making up stories in his own head about what is going on around him. And I should point out here that the root of this, at least in Saul's case, is his own sin that started it. His sinful actions against David (not to mention the LORD) started in motion a series of increasingly more twisted conspiracies that at the end of the day cause the man to consult a medium, call Samuel up from the dead, and end up in his own demise on a battlefield as he is run through with a sword. But let's continue with our little story.

Doeg the Edomite answers Saul, "I saw the son of Jesse coming to Nob, to Ahimelech the son of Ahitub, and he inquired of the LORD for him and gave him provisions and gave him the sword of Goliath the Philistine" (10). We have to pause here. There is one Psalm specifically said to be about Doeg—Psalm 52. It shares many things in common with Psalm 12, which many scholars also think has the context of Doeg in mind. There is curious conspiratorial language that runs throughout these psalms. The context of both is of liars, flatterers, deceitful people plotting away to destroy the godly. This is what people who conspire against others do.

In Doeg's response to Saul, he is bringing up the events from 1 Samuel 21. However, he is not recounting what happened properly. He makes it sound as if David and Ahimelech had a predetermined rendezvous. Instead, it tells us that when David came to Nob, Ahimelech came to meet him trembling and asked why he was alone (21:1). David then lied to Ahimelech because he was on the run. It was actually through deception that Ahimelech ended up giving David the food and sword. Did Doeg know this? All we know for certain is that he was there and saw the events.

It is clear when you come to chapter 22 that Doeg is in fact saying this to carry out his own conspiracy against Ahimelech. Doeg is playing on Saul's conspiratorial mind to his own evil ends! Saul sends a summons to Ahimelech and all his father's house and all the priests at Nob (22:11). Saul said to him, "Why have you conspired against me, you and the son of Jesse?" (13). Neither Ahimelech nor David were doing anything of the sort. David was on the run and the priest was in the dark.

At this point, the twisted mind of a king is in the full throes of a mind fractured by conspiracy theories of his own making and at the help of others. When the priest tries to explain the truth, that David is actually a faithful servant to the king (14) and knew nothing of any plot against him himself (15), the king's only reasonable response at such a heightened sense of conspiratorial insanity is to pronounce the death sentence upon Ahimelech (16). Doeg used that moment to strike and he killed 85 priests of God through his flattering, lying, deceitful lips.

What can we learn about conspiracy theories from Saul? We learn that often times, especially when a conspiracy theory seems to put oneself at the center of harm's way, it is often caused not by someone else, but by oneself.[41] We learn that it is easy to become entangled in an increasingly dark and sinister world of collusion and sedition where everyone is out to get you. We learn that our minds start to more easily listen to anything that will reinforce our already delusional beliefs. In short, we learn about some of the true dangers that can be associated with conspiracy theories.

---

[41] In my humble opinion, Alex Jones is a perfect case-study at the present time of someone exactly like this. I realize there are all kinds of conspiracy theories about Jones, but just watching the man over the years, it seems self-evident that his mind has cracked because everyone is out to get Alex.

Kings and Conspiracies

In this section, I want to look at how the ruling houses of Israel, over time, became filled with conspiracies. Throughout David's life and on into the kingly reigns of those who came after him, conspiracy became not the exception, but the rule. And where there are conspiracies, you can bet there are plenty of theories to go along with them.

- When David becomes king, his own son Absalom conspires against him (2Sa 15:12).
- When Nadab the son of Jeroboam became king in Israel, Baasha conspired against him (1Kg 15:27).
- When Elah the son of Baasha became king in Israel, his servant Zimri conspired against him (1Kg 16:8).
- When the troops found out about Zimri's conspiracy, they conspired against him and made Omri king (1Kg 16:16).
- Jehu the son of Jehoshaphat conspired against Joram (2Kg 9:14).
- Jehu conspired and killed all of Ahab's sons (2Kg 10:7).
- The servants of Joash committed a conspiracy together and struck him down in the house of Millo (2Kg 12:19).
- There was a conspiracy against Amaziah of Judah and he was murdered in Lachish (2Kg 14:19).
- Shallum the son of Jabesh conspired against Azariah king of Judah and killed him at Ibleam (2Kg 15:10).
- Menahem struck down king Shallum in a conspiracy (2Kg 15:14-15).
- Pekah conspired against king Pekahiah and killed him (2Kg 15:25).
- Hoshea conspired against Pekah and killed him (2Kg 15:30).
- The servants of Amon conspired against him and killed him in his own house (2Kg 21:23).
- The people of the land conspired against them and killed them for killing Amon (2Kg 21:24).

These are but a few of the verses that actually use the word "conspiracy" with regard to the intrigues of the courts of the kings of Israel and Judah, and they do not even begin to unravel lesser conspiracies that were taking place in virtually every reign of every king Israel and Judah ever had.

What can we learn from these? At least one thing is the way power is a magnet for conspiracy. So often, power comes to people because of the wicked things they have done to get it. They then become terrified of others, paranoid, all because they know what they have done to them! This in turn creates suspicion and distrust among virtually everyone. These things breed like flies and conspiracies become a plague across the land. One rational look at the modern world's power structure and it isn't hard to see that this is true whether we are talking about biblical times or the times we are living in today.

This is so much of today's politics in our modern world. It shouldn't have to be said that things are almost always like this at the highest levels. However, it seems to me that they do become worse and worse over time, and when you consider just how pervasive conspiracy theories are today, it is certainly not irrational to conclude that perhaps many of them are coming from actual conspiracies created by a multiplying wickedness that few people want to admit permeates our land. It is a frightful thing, especially considering how this all ended for God's chosen people in captivity in Babylon. How much worse it is for those who are not God's chosen people?

The Prophets and Conspiracies

There are three passages I would like to highlight in Israel's prophets. Amos tells us, "Then Amaziah the priest of Bethel sent to Jeroboam king of Israel, saying, 'Amos has conspired against you in the midst of the house of Israel. The land is not able to bear all his words'" (Amos 7:10). This is a fascinating piece of propagandizing manipulation, because it comes from one who is supposed to guard the law of God and the holy things of Israel. He tells the king a lie, that Amos is out to get him. In fact, it was not Amos who was lying, because the LORD was speaking through Amos. It was the LORD who was against Jeroboam (and Amaziah!). The conspiracy was not from the prophet, but from the one who said that the prophet was out to get the king. Oh, the lessons to be gained in the church from this one. How many soothsayers masquerading around as pastors and ministers of the gospel create conspiracies of their own minds that lead people away from the true words of the LORD?

Isaiah adds a warning about not buying into popular conspiracies. "Do not call conspiracy all that this people calls conspiracy" (Isa 8:12). It would be very easy to cherry-pick this verse and wrench it completely out of context, as if Isaiah is saying do not ever entertain any conspiracy theory ever. That isn't what it means. The verse adds, "Do not fear what they fear, nor be in dread." Edward Young has a helpful comment here,

> They were crying, "Conspiracy." But who was conspiring? It was Isaiah himself who had been attempting to dissuade Judah from seeking foreign aid. That was to go contrary to the policy of the court. Isaiah, Jeremiah and other prophets advocated a policy of dependence upon the Lord and not upon foreign powers. Surely that was treason! But Judah was the theocracy and should have been governed in all policies by God Himself. [42]

John Oswalt has a helpful application, which I think gets at the heart of all proper conspiratorial outworking as we try to think about these things biblically. "One possibility, when faced with potential calamities or disasters, is to forget God's sovereignty and proceed accordingly [e.g. conspiracies], but to do so is to invite calamity of a more profound nature, for God is the one fact we dare not overlook."[43] We've seen this theme before.

---

[42] Edward Young, *The Book of Isaiah, Chapters 1–18*, vol. 1 (Grand Rapids, MI: Wm. B. Eerdmans Publishing Co., 1965), 310.

[43] John N. Oswalt, *The Book of Isaiah, Chapters 1–39*, The New International Commentary on the Old Testament (Grand Rapids, MI: Wm. B. Eerdmans Publishing Co., 1986), 231.

Finally, consider Jeremiah. "The LORD said to me, 'A conspiracy exists among the men of Judah and the inhabitants of Jerusalem. They have turned back to the iniquities of their forefathers, who refused to hear my words. They have gone after other gods to serve them" (Jer 11:9-10). Jeremiah is using the same word (*qesher*) that Isaiah used. Young tells us that word means a conspiracy with treasonable intent! It is clear that Jeremiah does not contradict Isaiah. God wants Jeremiah to consider this conspiracy! It is the great conspiracy of all people—to turn from the living God, away from his grace, towards sin and foreign gods and corrupt powers. This is probably at the heart of almost every "conspiracy theory" as we know them today, be they little or huge in scope and plot.

The Conspiracy Against Messiah

The New Testament has conspiracies as well. For example, there is the conspiracy of forty Jewish leaders to have the Apostle Paul killed (Acts 23:12). There are also conspiracies that are of supernatural origin (going back to our discussion with Satan). The NT constantly warns against the "doctrines of demons" and "deceitful spirits." Their goal is subversion of the truth through infiltration of the church and the spreading of legalistic laws and lies or damning doctrines that pervert the pristine gospel of Jesus Christ. These are real conspiracies. So, it is no small matter that the Apostle tells us, "We do not wrestle against flesh and blood, but against the rulers, against the authorities, against the cosmic powers over this present darkness, against the spiritual forces of evil in the heavenly places" (Eph 6:12). Make no mistake, the fallen angels and their hideous demonic offspring mean to destroy the church at any cost.

All this biblical conspiring is demonstrated best in the one overarching conspiracy that begins way back at the Garden and is fulfilled in the Gospels. This is the Great Conspiracy of human history. It is committed by princes and principalities, angels and Adam's offspring alike. It is against the Messiah himself, God in flesh, Jesus Christ.

We saw that this conspiracy began in Eden with Satan who could not stand that some future seed of the woman would destroy him. I would argue that this is at the heart of the rebellion of the Watchers in Genesis 6 as well, for the whole point of God choosing Noah was that he was biologically pure, not tainted with any kind of unclean physical impurity like the Nephilim were.[44]

Psalm 2 takes us directly into the realm of prophecy. "Why do the nations conspire, and the peoples plot in vain" (Ps 2:1 RSV)? And it isn't just them. "The kings of the earth set themselves, and the rulers take counsel together" (2:2). The kings of the earth are set in contrast to the rulers/princes. The Greek word for "rulers" here is *archons*, and most of the time it is used in the NT it refers to the heavenly princes who rage against the LORD. My belief is that these are the Watchers of Genesis 6, including the "prince" of this world, Satan, and probably even the demonic hordes or at least their leaders. Everyone is in on this conspiracy. Against what or who?

"Against the LORD and against his Anointed" (2:2). They are conspiring against the heavenly Father and this holy Son. The NT quotes Psalm 2:7-8 perhaps more than any other passage. It is emphatic that this conspiracy was against Jesus. The baptism of Jesus and the transfiguration both echo the language "My Son." The Apostle Paul quotes this verse in a sermon saying that it directly foretold the coming of Jesus (Acts 13:33). Hebrews tells us that it is spoken not to the angels, but to Jesus Christ, the God-man (Heb 1:5; 5:5). So how does this conspiracy play itself out in the Gospels? I'll give you three different stages in Jesus' life that demonstrate it.

We've seen the first already, in John 8:44 when Jesus referred to Satan as the father of lies and murder. Gaebelein explains that "Our Lord testified of this character of the enemy [the Devil]

---

[44] Douglas Van Dorn, *Giants: Sons of the Gods* (Erie, CO: Waters of Creation Publishing, 2013), 36-38. This is the view given in 1 Enoch 106. For this, see the fascinating discussion in Andrew Collins, *From the Ashes of Angels: The Forbidden Legacy of a Fallen Race* (Rochester, VT: Bear & Co, 2001), 1-11.

when He spoke to those who conspired to kill Him."[45] Matthew is very clear about this conspiracy, and it happened rather early in Jesus' ministry. "The Pharisees went out and conspired against Him, as to how they might destroy Him" (Matt 12:14 NAS). Every question, every test, every word they spoke had Christ's demise as its ultimate goal. That's why Jesus told them even as early as John 8 when all they seemed to be doing was claiming that Abraham was their father, that they were really children of the devil.

It is near Jesus' appointed time to die that God allowed the conspiracy to blossom and flower. Matthew again tells us "Then the Pharisees went out and conspired to trap Jesus in His words" (Matt 22:15, Berean Study Bible). It was near this same time that Jesus harshly rebuked Peter, "Get behind me Satan" (Matt 16:23) and a little later that Satan entered into Judas (Luke 22:3). This is why it was important to talk about Satan at the beginning. Philip Ryken calls Satan "The ultimate Co-Conspirator" saying,

> Behind the betrayer there was a darker and more demonic in-fluence. To understand the true nature of the conspiracy that led to the crucifixion, we need to see that it came from the pit of hell. Luke begins his account of the clandestine encounter that Judas had with the chief priests by saying, "Then Satan entered into Judas called Iscariot, who was of the number of the twelve" (Luke 22:3). When he said this, Luke lifted the cur-tain of concealment to show that there was a supernatural di-mension to this conflict. There was a conspirator behind the conspiracy. He was the ultimate co-conspirator: Satan him-self—God's ancient enemy, the devil.[46]

This is what Psalm 2 is getting at when it says that everyone is in on the conspiracy.

---

[45] Arno C. Gaebelein, *Studies in Prophecy* (New York: Publication Office "Our Hope," 1918), 112–113.

[46] Philip Graham Ryken, *Luke*, ed. Richard D. Phillips, Philip Graham Ryken, and Daniel M. Doriani, vol. 2, Reformed Expository Commentary (Phillipsburg, NJ: P&R Publishing, 2009), 454.

Perhaps the craziest thing is that even though God lets them go through with their plans and they put Jesus to death, their conspiracy does not stop there. There was a little hitch in their scheming. They did not believe him when he said he would rise from the dead. He did. And they knew they were doomed. Thus, Matthew adds this important story near the end of his Gospel:

> And when they had assembled with the elders and taken coun-
> sel, they gave a sufficient sum of money to the soldiers and
> said, "Tell people, 'His disciples came by night and stole him
> away while we were asleep.' And if this comes to the gover-
> nor's ears, we will satisfy him and keep you out of trouble." So
> they took the money and did as they were directed. And this
> story has been spread among the Jews to this day.
>
> (Matt 28:12-15)

This is an incredibly informative story for our purposes, and it leads to a great conclusion to this chapter. They concocted a plan in secret. This plan was between people of power (guards and religious leaders). They devised it together. There were bribes that took place. Then, like a page written out of the CIA manual itself, they spread the disinformation and propaganda and it began to take hold in the minds and hearts of many people. Today, we would call that story a conspiracy theory! In this case, the conspiracy theory was a lie. In fact, it was a total lie.

Ironically, many NT scholars have argued that Matthew fabricated this story, that it couldn't possibly have been a real conspiracy by the Jews.[47] But how is this not its own conspiracy theory rooted in something like the same predisposed hatred of Jesus that Matthew tells us the Pharisees had towards Jesus? Those who doubt the Gospels' records about Jesus are constantly conspiring about how they can undermine its claims. It is crystal clear when you read liberal

---

[47] William Lane Craig, "The Guard at the Tomb," *New Testament Studies* 30 (1984): 273-81 gives several.

scholars talk about the resurrection that they will believe any conspiracy theory you throw their way, if they think it can overthrow Jesus still being alive today. This is the power of conspiracies in history and in the minds and hearts of those who believe them.

What we will turn to in the next chapter is a working textual case-study on how this ancient conspiracy against Christ by the Jewish rabbis did not end in the NT, but actually worked itself out in the form of tampering with the text long after the NT was finished being written, all in the hopes of keeping Jews from converting to Christianity. As we see today, both from the lack of knowledge people have about this, to the fact that so few Jews convert to Christianity like they did in the NT, this conspiracy has worked like a charm.

SUPPLEMENT TO
REPORT NO.

THIS IS UNEVALUATED INFORMATION

5

A TEXTUAL CONSPIRACY

TEXTUAL VARIANTS

SEVERAL CHAPTERS AGO, I discussed a fascinating textual variant in the book of Deuteronomy. Textual Variants are not well-known things, so let's spend a moment talking about what they are. Simply put, textual variants are differences in the texts of various ancient manuscripts. We are not used to such things, but why is that the case?

Some have suggested that the greatest invention in human history was the printing press. This single device made both the Renaissance and the Reformation possible. Both of those events, of course, changed the shape of world history. The printing press changed the way books were made. Rather than having to copy, by hand, the pages of a book, now a single page could be copied over and over and over again once the text type was put into place. Because it is copied by a machine, unless the original contained an error, there will not be errors in the copies. This is not true when people copy pages of books by hand. Humans make errors; humans make mistakes.

As a text is transmitted from one hand to the next, over generations you get what are called family trees of texts. This is because one place has one very ancient copy and it keeps using that and the family tree of copies to make new copies. Far away in another country, another ancient text of the same book will have been copied but not contain the same error. In this way and others, scholars are able to determine what the original text said, even though there are copying errors.

The errors I will look at in this chapter are from the Old Testament, which is a bit more complicated than the New Testament. The OT was originally written in Hebrew and some Aramaic. Our oldest copies of the full Hebrew text only go back to around 1000 AD. But the Hebrew text was also copied when it was translated into Greek and Aramaic and Ethiopian and so on. Our oldest copies of the OT are mostly in the Greek and this is due to no small degree to the discoveries at the Dead Sea. The Greek text, abbreviated as LXX (for the "seventy" translators that supposedly worked on it) is a translation of the Hebrew which was used quite often by the Apostles in the NT.

SONS OF GOD or sons of Israel?

Here is how the variant I discussed earlier reads in the English Standard Version. "When the Most High gave to the nations their inheritance, when he separated humankind, he set the bounds of the peoples according to the number of *the sons of God*."[48] This reading

---

[48] I have kept the [] out of this translation for ease of reading. Those refer to missing text that is filled in by other sources.

follows the oldest known texts that we have, those found at the Dead Sea. Where the Scrolls read "sons of God," the LXX usually reads "angels of God." In the Jewish Targums they are "the seventy angels, the princes of the nations." Believe it or not, we have a virtual parallel in Plato's *Critias* (yes, I said Plato). These are cited as gods such as Hephestus, Athena, and Poseidon.[49] Each of these are consistent with one another, for everywhere else the technical phrase "sons of God" is used in the Old Testament, it refers to heavenly beings, sometimes simply shortened to *elohim*, which is almost always translated as "gods."[50]

However, there is one variant that does not fit this at all. This is the reading as found in the Masoretic text. Rather than "sons of God," it reads, "sons of Israel." The question is, how can we account for this difference? Israel clearly is not a supernatural entity, save that it was given birth by God; but the people are just human, they are not supernatural entities. The easiest solution (and we see this verified when we look at the oldest manuscripts) is that some Rabbi, for whatever reason, when he was copying the sacred text, *interpreted* rather than transcribed the text as "Israel" instead of "God," probably justifying the change because Israel is sometimes called God's "son" (e.g. Ex 4:22). But why? It is incredibly rare to find the Jews changing the original text! If, as scholars argue, "sons of God" is the original reading, why would someone

---

[49] Compare for example, "Remember the days of old ... When the Most High gave to the nations their inheritance ... according to the number of the sons of God. But the LORD's [this must be the Son of God here] portion is ... Jacob his allotted heritage" (Deut 32:7-9) with "In the days of old the gods had the whole earth distributed among them by allotment ... Hephaestus and Athena ... took for their joint portion this land [Greece] ... Poseidon took for his allotment the island of Atlantis" (Plato, *Critias* 109c, 113c). On this uncanny similarity, many have said that Plato clearly came into contact with the Jews and the books of Moses. For example, Peter Allix, *The Judgment of the Ancient Jewish Church Against the Unitarians*, second edition (Oxford: Clarendon Press, 1821), 2; Justin Martyr, *Exhortation to the Greeks* 25).

[50] See Michael S. Heiser, "Deuteronomy 32:8 and the Sons of God," *Bibliotheca Sacra* 158:629 (Jan-Mar, 2001): 52-74.

do this? That's what the rest of his chapter seeks to investigate. And what a conspiracy theory this one is!

We need to begin with something we know from the writings of the Rabbis themselves was happening in the early days of Christianity. Simeon bar Yoḥai, a disciple of the school of famous Rabbi Akiva, writing sometime in the mid second century A. D., refers in the Genesis Rabbah to the "sons of God" as "sons of the nobility" and actually cursed anyone who called them "sons of God."[51] Taken in its best possible light, this seems to show that the reading of the Scrolls had either been lost or was believed to be unoriginal.

However, we have good reason to believe that something more was going on here. At some point, someone had to have changed the text and there has to be a rational explanation for it. The best explanation I've run across has to do with a raging rabbinical debate simultaneous to the life of Christ among Jews that there were, in their words, "two powers in heaven."[52] The idea was that while there is one God ("Hear O Israel, the LORD your God, the LORD is one; Deut 6:4), there were actually two (or perhaps more) powers in heaven. Like God himself, the second power was often called Yahweh. Yahweh is the God of Israel and Israel has only one God; yet there is more than one Yahweh!

For example, they vigorously debated texts like Genesis 19:24, "Then the LORD [Yahweh] rained on Sodom and Gomorrah sulfur and fire from the LORD [Yahweh] out of heaven." Some taught that there were two Yahwehs in this verse, one on earth and one in heaven. By the way, the Church Fathers seized in mass upon this text and used it as a proof-text that this passage clearly taught the Father and Son. Well, many Jews had similar

---

[51] See GenRab 26:5. *Genesis Rabbah: The Judaic Commentary to the Book of Genesis: A New American Translation*, Trans. Jacob Neusner (BJS 104; Atlanta: Scholars Press 1985), 282.

[52] See especially Alan Segal, *Two Powers in Heaven: Early Rabbinic Reports about Christianity and Gnosticism* (Boston, Brill Academic Pub, 2002).

opinions even before Jesus came along, they simply used the language of "power" rather than "Son."

There wasn't really too much of a problem with this, as both those who affirmed and denied the second power were regarded as "within the pale" of orthodox Judaism. Until, that is, someone named Jesus of Nazareth came along. In one particular instance, Jesus confronts the Pharisees and quotes Psalm 82:6 to them. "Is it not written in your Law, 'I said, you are gods?'" The common interpretation these days says Jesus is telling the Pharisees that the OT somehow refers to them (i.e. the rulers of Israel) as "gods."[53] This makes little sense of the context, as if Jesus is saying, "Look fellas, I'm a god, you're a god, can't we all just get along?" Besides, this citation only intensified their hatred of him, and John makes it clear that through it, Jesus was claiming for himself divinity. Indeed, Jesus goes on to do more than that, for he says that he and the Father are one.[54]

But it makes perfect sense of the two-powers context, if Jesus is claiming that he is one of the heavenly sons of God who has now come into their midst. They would have understood that he was basically claiming to be the Angel of the LORD, the second Yahweh infleshed. If they didn't believe that, such a claim would certainly create such a hatred that it might lead to murder, especially if he was attacking your own religious authority.

Strange Genealogies

[53] In fact, this was the view that prevailed among the "orthodox" rabbis when they officially made two-powers theology a heresy. Hence, we find for example Symmachus (c. 170 A.D.) translating the expression "sons of God" as "the sons of the rulers." See the short discussion in Jacob Johannes Theodoor Doedens, "The Sons of God in Genesis 6:1-4" (Ph.D. diss. Theologische Universiteit Kampen, 2013), 92-93.

[54] See Michael Heiser, "You've Seen One Elohim, You've Seen Them All? A Critique of Mormonism's Use of Psalm 82," *FARMS Review* 19/1 (2007): 221–266. I have also dealt with this extensively in my sermons on John 10 and Psalm 82 found at our website www.rbcnc.com.

Genesis 11

Let's take this discussion now to a very different kind of textual variant. This one is found in of all things one of the genealogies of Genesis. At first it seems wholly benign, unimportant,
worth almost no attention at all. The following discussion was
inspired from a *YouTube* video titled, "Were the Pyramids Built
Before the Flood?"[55]

The Hebrew and Greek LXX give two different timelines for
post-Flood history. The Hebrew Masoretic text that we have is not
the original Hebrew text, but a copy of a copy of a copy. Our best
and earliest copy of this is the Leningrad Codex copied in 1008
A.D. The LXX predates this by over 1,000 years, but it is in Greek.
Many people are under the faulty assumption that because it isn't
the original language, the Greek translation must necessarily be
inferior. But this is a mistake. Let's see why using a genealogy.

Arphaxad	35	135	135	135
Shelah	30	130	130	130
Eber	34	134	134	134
Peleg	30	130	130	130
Reu	32	132	132	132
Serug	30	130	130	130
Nahor	29	79	79	?

Genesis 11 is the genealogy of Shem to Abram. In that list
of names, dates are given for how old each man was when he bore
the son that the lineage follows (see chart above). In the Masoretic
text, which most English Bibles follow, the ages are all in their
30s. However, in the LXX, the ages are all in their 130s. Curiously,

55 Nathan Hoffman, "Where the Pyramids Built Before the Flood? (Masoretic
Text vs. Original Hebrew)," *YouTube* (May 28, 2017),
https://www.youtube.com/watch?v=VI1yRTC6kGE.

the Samaritan Pentateuch and Josephus, of which we have copies that far predate the Leningrad Codex, follow the LXX.

If you plot this out on a graph, you find that the Hebrew text forces you to believe that Shem outlived all but one of his sons and was in fact a contemporary of Abraham, even though he was the biological son of Noah! That's pretty astonishing. From this, it has become fairly common for people to tell you that Shem knew Abraham.

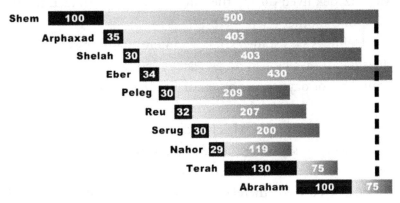

Graphs are screen shots taken from the Hoffman video

But, if you take the timeline of the other three witnesses, it doesn't look anything at all like this. Instead, an extra 600 years of post-Flood history are added to the timeline creating a very different looking graph.

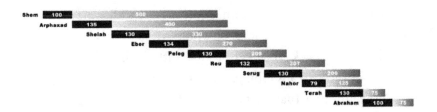

In this case, Shem dies hundreds of years prior to Abraham, which is what you would expect. The obvious question becomes, why would a Jewish scribe drop the "hundred" from six different names, thereby lessening biblical history by over 600 years? The only answer that makes sense to me is actually completely mind-blowing.

According to Nathan Hoffman, the author of the video I referenced, he thinks this was done deliberately in order to help disprove what Hebrews says about Jesus being the Great High Priest. As Hebrews, taking its cue from Psalm 110 says, Jesus is the Great High Priest according to the priesthood of Melchizedek. Now, Melchizedek lived during the time of Abraham. In fact, the two knew one another (Gen 14:18-19).

Hebrews says some extremely interesting things about Melchizedek. It says he had no genealogy, no father, no mother, no beginning of days, and no end of life (Heb 7:3). It further says that Jesus is like Melchizedek in that his priesthood continues forever (3, 24) and like Melchizedek has an "indestructible life" (16). Finally, it says that the Levites received tithes because they were "mortal men" (8), seemingly in contradistinction to Melchizedek who must therefore be immortal. All of this fits right into some Jewish speculation that Melchizedek was in fact God (I would say, the Angel of the LORD).[56]

Here is where the thinking cap has to be put on. Consider this hatred of Jesus by the Rabbis that we have discussed. At the very least, Hebrews in using this kind of language, is making a connection to Jesus being immortal. I would argue that it is actually pointing to an organic essential connection between Melchizedek and Jesus that goes beyond the level of typology. To put it another way, Jesus is Melchizedek, the Son of God infleshed. Either way, the point is the same to a Rabbi. Jesus is immortal.

Now consider that we have some fairly early interpretations from the Rabbis that Melchizedek is actually Shem, the son of

---

[56] For example, 11Q13 Melchizedek Text 2.13-16 in the Dead Sea Scrolls; Ps 110:5 LXX; 2 Enoch (A) 71:27-29.

Noah.[57] We know Shem's father and mother were Noah and his wife. We know his genealogy, his birth as well as his death. The thinking then is, if Shem actually is Melchizedek, then this disproves the language Hebrews uses and therefore destroys the argument that Jesus is the Great High Priest.

The problem is, on the original reading of the timeline, Shem died hundreds of years before Abraham and therefore cannot be Melchizedek. Every Rabbi certainly would have known this. So what's the solution? Take a totally innocuous passage, just a bunch of numbers that no one cares about, and drop off the "hundreds." Voilà! Shem now overlaps Abraham and we can argue that he was Melchizedek. In the words of the immortal Connect Four commercial, "Pretty sneaky, sis."

Hoffman brings up another point that is relevant to our discussion. Paul makes this strange comment, warning the Christians not to get involved with Jews in myths and endless genealogies (compare 1Tim 1:4; 4:7; 2Tim 4:4; Tit 1:14). I don't think Paul is talking about "mythology," for that is more the realm of the Gentiles. I think he is talking about conspiracy theories, conspiracies that were created by the Rabbis in order to try to disprove the divinity of Jesus Christ, even to the point that they were willing to tamper with sacred Scripture itself.

Genesis 46:27 and Parallel Texts

This discussion takes us to one final variant I want to discuss. Hoffman brings this up at the end of his video, however, he does not seem to be aware of the direct connection this has with our Deuteronomy 32:8 variant or to the two-powers controversy. Thus, we can add something more to what he says.

We will start in Acts 7:14 in the famous last sermon of the martyr Stephen. He says, "Then Joseph sent and called his father

---

[57] Seder Olam 21, Targum Neofiti Gen 14:18; Abot deR. Natan (A) 2.

Jacob and all his relatives to him, seventy-five people." Ok, no big deal, right? Let's look at the OT roots of this number.

Genesis 46:27 in the Hebrew Masoretic text tells us, "And the sons of Joseph, who were born to him in Egypt, were two. All the persons of the house of Jacob who came into Egypt were seventy." The same number "70" appears in Exodus 1:5 as well. However, when you go to the LXX, the number is 75, not 70. This is consistent with Stephen. Furthermore, the LXX of Exodus 1:5 also reads 75 (they did not find any copies of Genesis 46:27 at the Dead Sea).

How is this relevant to Deuteronomy 32:8? Consider the Targum of Jonathan of this verse. "When the Most High made allotment of the world unto the nations which proceeded from the sons of Noah, in the separation of the writings and languages of the children of men at the time of the division, He cast the lot among *the seventy angels, the princes of the nations* with whom is the revelation to oversee the city." Now, the same targum concludes that it was seventy souls who went down to Israel and is seemingly trying to harmonize two disparate and contradictory views. But the key is the seventy angels. You see, seventy was according to all the ancient traditions of the Jews and even of the Canaanites, the number of the sons of God—the heavenly beings.

A Word about Giants

Since some of my readers are familiar with my work on giants in the Bible—those guys called the Nephilim in Genesis 6:4 and Numbers 13:33, or the Rephaim and other terms in places like Genesis 14 or Deuteronomy 2, I want to flesh out one more implication of this Rabbinical change to the meaning of the "sons of God" which is directly related to conspiracy theories.

Just a couple of minutes ago I got a random question from a friend, a Ph.D. professor in OT, asking me a question about giants. After I answered his question, and he responded with "holy cow," he then told me, "Anytime a person brings this stuff up, it feels like it just breaks the walls of the Western church. I seriously cannot help but feel like I'm in conspiracy mode when I get close to this topic." He was wondering aloud with me how a person can help themselves get out of this mode of thinking. My solution is, you have to understand the history of this subject.

There is a reason why giants in the Bible feel conspiratorial. There actually *was* a conspiracy, but not from whom you think and not in what you might expect. More on that in a moment. It is not a coincidence that two of the variants discussed above circulate around Deuteronomy 32:8. "Sons of God" is found there and the number "seventy" is circulating in the background of this verse, as the Targum demonstrated. The former of these is directly related to giants; the latter is indirectly related to giants in that it was the known number across the Middle East associated with these divine sons of God.

Genesis 6:2 tells us that the sons of God saw the daughters of men (Adam) and vs. 4 adds that these women gave birth to the Nephilim. Obviously, if "sons of God" are perfectly human, so much for any kind of strange supernatural interpretation. What's curious is the history of interpretation on who the Nephilim were and how it corresponds directly to the changes made in our textual variants, which both seem to be traceable to around the second century A.D.

As Jaap Doedens has meticulously shown in his Ph.D. dissertation on the sons of God,[58] the universal interpretation of the sons of God in Jewish circles until the second century A.D. was that they were supernatural entities. This includes the tradition found in all the Targums, Philo, Josephus, 1 Enoch, 2 Enoch, Jubilees, The Testament of the Twelve Patriarchs, 2 Baruch, and the Dead Sea Scrolls. In Christian circles, it was again the universal interpretation, with the exception of one historian who leaves

---

[58] Jacob J. T. Doedens, "The Sons of God in Genesis 6:1-4," Ph.D. Dissertation Theologische Universiteit Kampen (2013). http://theoluniv.ub.rug.nl/32/7/2013Doedens%20Dissertation.pdf.

open the possibility of the supernatural interpretation because he was dealing with the textual variant, until 350 AD.[59] This includes Justin Martyr, Athenagoras, Irenaeus, Clement of Alexandria, Bardaisan of Edessa, The Pseudo-Clementine Literature, Tertullian, Origen, Cyprian, Commodian, Methodius, Lactantius, Alexander of Lycopolis, Eusebius, Cyril of Jerusalem, Ambrosius, Sulpicius Severus, and I would strongly argue Jude, 1 Peter, 2 Peter, and 1 Corinthians (the head covering verse). So how does a centuries long monolithic interpretation change overnight? The answer is directly related to the subtle change in numbers in the genealogies, and to the change of language from sons of God to sons of Israel. Simply put, there was a conspiracy.

The conspiracy was of Jewish origins, and I'm not trying to be anti-Semitic here. This is known history. The Rabbis changed these texts and reinterpreted the Nephilim, along with changing the actual text in the other variants, are you ready for it … because of Jesus. This is hardly my own theory. Secular scholars from Alan Segal to Christian scholars like Michael Heiser made similar arguments before me. Here is Heiser summarizing the point,

> That acceptance changed when certain Jews, the early Christians, connected Jesus with this orthodox Jewish idea. This explains why these Jews, the first converts to following Jesus the Christ, could simultaneously worship the God of Israel and Jesus, and yet refuse to acknowledge any other god. Jesus was the incarnate second Yahweh. In response, as Segal's work demonstrated, Judaism pronounced the two powers teaching a heresy sometime in the second century A.D.[60]

---

[59] Doedens, Jacob J. T. "The Indecent Descent of the Sethites: The Provenance of the Sethites-Interpretation of Genesis 6:1-4." *Sárospataki Füzetek* 16:3–4 (2012): 47–57. https://www.academia.edu/17793988/The_Indecent_Descent_of_the_Sethites_T he_Provenance_of_the_Sethites-Interpretation_of_Genesis_6_1-4.

[60] Michael Heiser, "Two Powers in Heaven," *Dr Michael S Heiser*, https://drmsh.com/the-naked-bible/two-powers-in-heaven/.

You see, the Rabbis knew that Jesus was claiming to be the "son of God." They knew that he was claiming to be one of the "sons of God" from Psalm 82 (see John 10:34), but more, that he was claiming to be Yahweh who inherited Israel in Deuteronomy 32:9, for since it is the sons of God who inherit in the previous verse, Yahweh in vs. 9 can only be the Son and not the Father who inherits this nation.

Therefore, they concocted a way for the translation "sons of Israel" to make more sense. They were doing everything in their power, while still having some kind of theological justification, to eliminate any loophole the Christians might "find" in the Hebrew Scripture, for claiming that a person could be both God and man. Since everyone knew that the number was seventy, they changed the number of sons who went down into Israel from 75 to 70 and presto! Now they had a textual hinge upon which to peg their novel translation of the sons of God. Suddenly, there was no reason one had to take the Nephilim as being supernatural hybrids, since the phrase could mean non-supernatural people like Israel, so that could go too. All this, because that's how badly they hated their Messiah who came to them. But that's what we saw in the last chapter, isn't it? The ultimate conspiracy of men is to try to somehow overturn the Father's rule through the Lord Jesus Christ.

This is the power of conspiracy theories. They can distort and twist everything, to the point where even God himself is not off limits. Furthermore, they can create great confusion for generations to come. My friend believed that it was the supernatural view that caused him to enter into the world of conspiracies. The reality is the opposite. It is the anti-supernatural view of the sons of God and the Nephilim that originated in the Rabbis that was the true conspiracy. I believe the Christians unwittingly adopted a rabbinical view of the Nephilim, as their novel theory worked its way outward from its source and began to lose its Jewish origins to the sands of time.

Conspiring in unique ways against the Triune God, of course, has never stopped. We have entire movements throughout history that are in one form or other conspiracies against the True and Living God and his written word. Gnosticism, perhaps itself formed out of bizarre mixing Jewish Kabballah, biblical Christianity, Greek Philosophy, and just plain old conspiratorial plotting, insists that the Creator Yahweh is an evil masculine demiurge, a "fool" born of the rebellious Aeon Sophia, who is herself of the a handful of divine emanations of the "True God," which is androgynous! This *deeply* sexually perverted religion insists that Yahweh is the creator of this world, but he is an evil trickster. He goes around telling people that he is the only God, when in fact there are many more that are higher than himself. Curiously, the Logos is viewed as much higher than Yahweh, so when Jesus is called the Logos, he becomes this strange neither-God-nor-man spirit-guide who is supposed to lead us all to the True Light. Of course, he does anything but in Gnostic literature.

Perhaps the most popular peddler of Gnostic conspiracies today is Dan Brown who wrote *The DaVinci Co*de, and along with *Angels & Demons* and *Inferno* have become box-office smash hits starring Tom Hanks—himself the subject of not a few conspiracy theories. Brown has, for example, popularized the conspiracy theory that Jesus and Mary Magdalene ended up getting married and having royal babies that founded the Merovingian dynasty of France. And people gobble it up, all while claiming that the *real* conspiracy was Constantine and those evil orthodox bishops who squashed the truth at Nicaea so that they could all get rich and powerful as the expense of the truth Gnostic religion. Cults like this subvert biblical words and ideas so that they can pervert biblical truth and its utterly unique God. It is crafty and shrewd. Truly, Psalm 2 continues to show itself true. The peoples of the earth conspire together against the LORD and against his Anointed. No wonder it says, "Kiss the Son lest you perish in your way."

EVALUATING CONSPIRACY THEORIES

The Big Lie

 N HER EXCELLENT TED X TALK on media manipulation of things like the claims that drug companies make, Sharyl Attiksson, five-time Emmy Award winner and RTNDA Edward R. Murrow Award recipient for outstanding journalism with CBS News asks a very important question about the "reality" around you,

> What if what you discovered was false? A carefully constructed narrative by unseen special interests designed to manipulate your opinion? A Truman-showeque alternate reality all around you? Complacency in the news media combined

with incredibly powerful propaganda and publicity forces mean we sometimes get little of the truth.[61]

Propaganda is information of a biased or misleading nature that is used to promote or publicize a particular political cause or point of view. We've seen how the CIA openly engages in it. They learned from the masters, many of whom became leading members of this and many other organizations in the United States after WWII, when our nation refused to put most of these wicked men to death, but instead chose to assimilate them and their "findings" into the American military industrial complex.

Adolf Hitler famously wrote in *Mein Kampf* about what he called "the big lie." This is a lie so huge that the "broad masses of a nation" become easy prey to it because, though they lie in little matters themselves, they would "be ashamed to resort to large-scale falsehoods. It would never come into their heads to fabricate colossal untruths, and they would not believe that others could have the impudence to distort the truth so infamously."[62]

At the end of the war, Hermann Göring, the second in command of the Third Reich behind only Hitler himself, was taken into custody by the Allied armies and was sent to the Nuremburg trials. During those trials, in 1946, he candidly made the following statement.

Naturally, the common people don't want war; neither in Russia nor in England nor in America, nor for that matter in Germany. That is understood. But, after all, it is the leaders of the country who determine the policy and it is always a simple matter to drag the people along, whether it is a democracy or a fascist dictatorship or a Parliament or a Communist dictatorship ... voice or no voice, the people can always be brought to the bidding of the leaders. That is easy. All you

---

[61] Sharyl Attiksson, "Astroturf and Manipulation of Media Messages," *TEDxUniversityofNevada* (Feb 6, 2015), https://www.youtube.com/watch?v=-bYAQ-ZZtEU.
[62] Adolf Hitler, *Mein Kampf*, trans. James Murphy (London: Hurst and Blackett, 1939), 185.

have to do is tell them they are being attacked and denounce the pacifists for lack of patriotism and exposing the country to danger. It works the same way in any country.[63]

Joseph Goebbels who was in charge of Hitler's "Ministry of Propaganda" (yes, they actually called it that) is supposed to have said, "A lie told once is only a lie, but if you tell it a thousand times, it becomes the truth," and "If you tell the same lie enough times, people will believe it. And the bigger the lie, the better."[64] He called people simple creatures, "primitive." Therefore, propaganda has to be simple and repetitive. What was *his* message? What did he hammer home over and over and over again to the German people? That all of the problems in society were because of the Jews. It's an absurd claim, a lie. But it worked. Because propaganda done right, works. Every time. Not on every individual, but on a mass scale. Lies work. People believe them.

There are many ends you can have in mind that you want a population to believe. There are many ways you can dupe a population into believing whatever you want them to believe about a thing. Propaganda in our very own country has and will continue to happen. It is only a person's own personal conspiracy theory that it doesn't happen that keeps them from seeing this openly admitted truth.

But let's say you have been convinced it is true. What then? How can you wade through the lies and deceptions both in what you are being told from an "official" source and in what you hear in competing conspiracy theories? In this chapter, I want to help you think about what makes a conspiracy theory worth pursuing or not. My goal here is to help you—as you come across something you have never heard about before—to begin making

---

[63] G. M. Gilbert, *Nuremberg Diary* (New York: Signet Book, 1947), 255-56.

[64] It is not known whether Goebbels literally said this. He certainly said other things like it, it falls in line with Hitler and Göring, and time has attached this to his name.

evaluations about its possible validity. This question orbits around the idea of "truth."

Conspiracy Theories and Truth

Coherence and Conspiracies

In philosophy, there are basically two theories of truth that compete for first place. The first theory is called the *coherence theory of truth*. In this theory, our knowledge of a thing is justified by how well its relationship to all other possible related beliefs cohere to one another. To put it another way, a thing is true if it is internally consistent rather than contradictory. Is it sound on all the points it addresses? For me, this is one of the first things I look for in a conspiracy theory. Is it constant with itself and with other things outside of the theory to which it speaks, or it is full of logical holes and essentially irrational?

It is important to distinguish here facts from reasoning to a conclusion from the facts. All conspiracy theories are rooted in facts; usually hundreds or even thousands of them. But the facts themselves have to be true. I always check facts, not on every detail, but on random things I think the person I'm hearing wouldn't think I would check.

A related thing here is how people love to look for patterns and anomalies in things they think are "off." It isn't bad to look for patterns, especially when something really is off! But sometimes, it can just be the human tendency to see animals in clouds or faces in bathroom tile. We are pattern finders, even if they aren't done deliberately; even if they aren't real. We have to beware of this tendency, because it is easy to fool ourselves with our own ingenuity. When we see enough facts and/or patterns that it becomes overwhelming, we make inductions to help form a coherent theory. That theory needs to use critical thinking and be logically reasonable and consistent.

One of the appeals of many conspiracy theories is their internal consistency. I'll tell you, I'm writing this portion of the book on Good Friday and to this moment, the Q conspiracy theory is, of all the theories out there, including and especially the "official" story, the most internally consistent theory I've seen. It is one of the things that makes it so fascinating, all the more because it is so unbelievably complex, I have no idea how someone would make it up.

If you've ever watched a show like *Breaking Bad*, you see what happens when a person begins to lie. They add lie upon lie upon lie. Soon, their entire created world (a conspiracy theory meant to contradict reality) that they spin to everyone else, collapses under the inconsistency of its own weight. Too many holes make the lie easy to discover. The same is true with a conspiracy theory. The more holes in it, the easier it is (or should be) to figure out that it isn't worth spending a lot of time on.

Correspondence and Conspiracies

But coherence is not the main view of truth, mostly because it gives a necessary but not sufficient account of things. There are plenty of ideas that are internally consistent but totally untrue. This is why *Breaking Bad* works. Walter White's lies seem true ... for a while. Thus, the other dominate view is that truth is what *corresponds to reality*. In other words, it is real.

One of the things that makes most conspiracy theories so frustrating is that there never seems to be a way of finding out if the thing corresponds to reality or not. It might be perfectly coherent, but that isn't enough. I want to know if it is real. Of course, part of the glamour and allure of a conspiracy theory is that answering this question it is often just barely out of reach. Like a season-ending cliff-hanger, that's what keeps people coming back for more. And, I'll admit, that does make them fun.

Let me return to Q for a moment as I think about this question further. While looking into Q from almost the beginning, I quickly gave it up because it was just too overwhelming. I didn't have the time or energy for it. Plus, I hate riddles! Man, do I hate riddles. That scene in the Hobbit with Bilbo and Gollum going at it? Now *that* is frustrating for me. That's Q!

But I came back to it the last few or so weeks. There are two main reasons for this. First, I found that this thing has begun to encompass many of the other theories under its huge canopy. JFK, 9-11, Anthrax, Bohemian Grove, the Illuminati … it's all here under Q. And that's a fascinating thing. How can anyone have come up with this? Second, and more importantly, I quickly discovered from the *anons* who had been deciphering Q drops and, quite frankly, from the President himself who is clearly using Q (to what end, we do not yet know), that Q is a falsifiable conspiracy theory.

Falsifiability and Conspiracies

Falsifiability is one of the most important tests that a scientific hypothesis can have. Falsifiability means that on its own terms, you can demonstrate scientifically that the theory is true or not, or at least that it corresponds to everything you know at the time. Q has become that. You see, the idea is that within the near future, without date setting, but within a month or a season, what is said will come to pass or it won't. There is no second chance here. Nor can it last on into the eternal future. Many were convinced that Easter would be a good test. Others, the end of April. But everyone knows that if this goes into the summer and fall that the theory is simply wrong, or at least that everyone has decoded the information improperly. For me, it is pretty obvious that if it is wrong, it needs to be dumped. Now that's a theory I can have fun with and that perhaps I can even learn a thing or two about the world from, because there is something more than just scaring myself that is up for grabs.

If a theory isn't falsifiable now, it doesn't mean that it can't become so in the future. Again, Q is a good example. For the last three years, I do not believe it was at that point. Most conspiracy theories never get to the place of being falsifiable. But if Q is right, all of those mentioned above and more will be! That makes it even more interesting to me.

But if there is no possible way that a conspiracy theory could ever be proven true, I believe we need to place it in a category in our minds that allows us to think much less seriously about it. Let them be amazing stories that *could* be true, but we'll never know. If that's in your thinking, I believe it can certainly help with many of the detrimental effects such things can have on all of us.

There is one thing to beware of here. Beware of saying that you or someone who agrees with you are the only ones who could verify or falsify a conspiratorial hypothesis. Take again the flat-earth movement. These people have given tests that they say would prove the theory true. And yet, those same tests have, according to a good many people, already been carried out ... hundreds and thousands of times. The problem is, those holding the conspiracy theory that the earth is flat think they are all lying.

It is dangerous to be so committed to a theory that no one holding the opposite view could ever prove it false to your satisfaction. Just today a meme came across my desk that reads, "I'm not convinced we landed on the moon. I mean, think about how many moons you believe we HAVEN'T landed on. Thousands. I just go one further." #Skepticism. Then the reply, "I'm willing to believe if there's enough evidence. However you can't use any evidence provided by NASA, as that would be biased information. Of course THEY'RE going to say that they landed on the moon. No, to convince me you need to show me proof from a source that believes that NASA DIDN'T land on the moon. Only then will I believe you." Haha. This is actually a dig at atheists who refuse to let the Bible have a say in the existence of God, but that's exactly what I'm talking about here. You need to be self-aware enough to see if you are so committed to a theory that you can't be proven wrong unless you yourself confirm it.

Just here I am also reminded of the story of Doubting Thomas after the resurrection. Thomas had heard for more than a week that Jesus had been raised from the dead. In fact, Jesus *had* been raised from the dead. But he thought it was a conspiracy theory. He had told the other Disciples, "Unless I see in his hands the mark of the nails, and place my finger into the mark of the nails, and place my hand into his side, I will never believe" (John 20:25). In other words, the word of his friends wasn't proof enough! Just think of the audacity; Jesus' resurrection could only be proven true or false by Thomas! That's an amazing thing.

Sometime later, Jesus came into the room where Thomas and the others were gathered together. The risen Lord said in the presence of all, "Peace be with you" (26). Jesus, showing his omniscience (for he was not there when Thomas made that bold declaration to the other disciples), commanded Thomas to put his finger here and see his hands and to place his hand in his side. Then he commanded him not to disbelieve, but to believe (27). This was an amazing act of Christ, condescending in grace, to a man who was certain the others were conspiring in some kind of insane lie. But God isn't very often that gracious. While we may have good reasons not to trust others, we also need to have some kind of trust for those who disagree with us. If we do not, we risk being Thomas and the Lord may in fact not ever come to us with such an offer and then we run the risk of living in our own delusional world forever.

Circularity and Conspiracies

One of the dangers of conspiracy theories is their *circularity*. Circular reasoning is when A is true because of B and B is true because of A. Thomas was in this circle. Jesus hasn't risen because he hadn't proven it. He can't prove it because you guys (those disciples) are delusional, he hasn't risen. This is one of the problems with a coherence theory of truth. A is true because of B might be perfectly rational. And B is true because of C might be perfectly consistent. Add in another 100 of these and you get a very complex set of consistent arguments. But at the end of the day, If Z is true because of A, it is a circle and a thing simply can't be true proven true by a circular argument. Something needs to be outside of the argument, in the real world.

Related to this, another problem with conspiracy theories is that they seem to multiply like rabbits. This is because when a thing can't be proven true, if you add more evidence through other related conspiracy theories, it gives the impression that it must be true. For example, someone thinks that JFK wasn't shot by one person. Instead of finding evidence, they turn to the assassination of his brother. Then they add on the assignation of Malcom X and Martin Luther King Jr. The idea is that the more people you add who were assassinated, it must prove that JFK wasn't killed by just one person. Now, it might be true that JFK wasn't killed by just one person, but these other assassinations only add confusion to that point. They do not add much by way of corroborating evidence. They just make the circle bigger. It is quite common to hear people constantly say about these things, "Could it really all just be a coincidence?"

Well, yes, it actually could. Today I was watching someone talk about a terrible murder of a little girl that took place near the famous ancient rock called Ayers Rock in the middle of nowhere Australia. The man had discovered that a terrible Satan worshiping witch (she really is one) just "happened" to be there at the same time as this child was killed. "Coincidence?" Of course not! But then, as I was watching his video, I got a call from a friend. Unbelievably, he told me that my good friend, a man who had been a POW in WWII who had been in an Alzheimer's home in recent days passed away yesterday, Easter Sunday morning.

The man's wife was still alive (they had been married for over 75 years!). They were scrambling about how to tell her and after a few hours went over to where she had been staying in recent days only to find that she had died just a couple of hours after him, also on Easter morning. That's an incredibly story. "Coincidence?" Was there some plot here? Were they murdered by Nazis in their sleep? No. I do believe God was incredibly gracious to them both and had his own story to tell. But sometimes incredible things really do happen and nothing nefarious is involved.

All of this results in a warning. When considering conspiracy theories, think about its scientific plausibility. Consider its coherence, its circularity, its falsifiability. Be careful. Use your brain. Keep thinking. Always ask questions, especially if you are convinced it is true. In doing this, you will be on solid footing and there will be no legitimate way someone could call you crazy.

Astroturfing & False Flags:

This leads nicely to my next main point. One of the deeply concerning things about the whole field of conspiracy theories is how they are so often spoken about. Again, we've seen how the CIA actually had a lot to do with this change of opinion about them. One modern phenomenon related to this is something called astroturfing. I've mentioned it a couple of times, but I'm guessing most have never heard of it.

What is astroturfing? Well, it isn't when professionals went into the Houston Astrodome and re-turfed the field! Technically speaking, it is the new form of professional paid D. C. lobbying, usually done by huge corporations like drug companies to blur the truth of studies and facts beyond recognition. Though not (officially) related to groups like the CIA, it nevertheless bears a good deal in common with gray PSYOPs. And that makes them a form of conspiracy. But I assure you, astroturfing is no conspiracy theory, though, of course, they want you to think that it is.

Attkisson's talk on propaganda defines astroturfing as, "A perversion of grassroots, as in fake grassroots. Astroturf is when political, corporate, or other special interests disguise themselves and publish blogs, start Facebook and Twitter accounts, publish ads and letters to the editor, or simply post comments online to try to fool you into thinking an independent or grassroots movement is speaking."[65] It is done on social media, Wikipedia, by starting non-profits and conducting "studies" and then manipulating Google search engines so that you will find them, and so on. If they think it is something you will read or listen to, they've got their dirty little fingers in it. And they go after anyone who tries to report them or defy them. She explains, "The whole point of astroturfing is to give the impression that there's widespread support for or against an agenda when there's not. Astroturf seeks to manipulate you into changing your opinion by making you feel as if you're an outlier when you're not."

Attiksson asks an important question related to conspiracy theories. "So now you may be thinking, 'What can I do? I thought I'd done my research. What chance do I have separating fact from fiction, especially if seasoned journalists with years of experience can be so easily fooled?'" This question relates directly to conspiracy theories. There's a one-to-one relationship here. Her answer is very important to understand. Here are some of her strategies to help you recognize signs of propaganda and astroturf, and when you know what you are looking for, you start to see it *everywhere*. Hallmarks include:

- *Use of inflammatory language* such as "crank," "quack," "nutty," "lies," "paranoid," "pseudo," and "conspiracy." These are her terms, and how easily they can be transferred over to the world of conspiracy theories. These are the very kinds of phrases so often thrown around this world too. She even used the word

---

[65] This and the following list come from her TEDx Talk.

"conspiracy" as "inflammatory language." And, in fact, the way "conspiracy theory" is used today, it is itself very often inflammatory language. Attkisson gets it!

- *Astroturfers often claim to debunk myths that aren't myths at all.* To put that another way, they create conspiracy theories in order to debunk reality. "What if the whole notion of the myth is itself a myth, and you and [others] fell for it."

- *Beware when interests attack an issue by controversializing or attacking the people*, personalities, and organizations surrounding it, rather than addressing the facts. In the world of conspiracy theories, we could translate this into attacking popular people associated with the theory or simply attacking the theory as a theory without addressing the facts of the theory. This is all classic logical fallacy stuff like the Bandwagon, Appeal to Authority, Ad Hominem fallacies.

- *Astroturfers tend to reserve all of their public skepticism for those exposing wrongdoing rather than wrongdoers.* Instead of questioning authority, they question those who question authority. Moved into the world of conspiracy theories, rather than questioning the official story being a good thing, it is the worst possible thing you could engage in, and they let you know it.

When you see these things, you know that you are near the astroturfer's home field. Beware. For the same kinds of tactics are used all the time to mock, ridicule, debunk, and otherwise keep people from entertaining "conspiracy theories."

Similar to Attkisson, Richard Dolan has done some fine work thinking through False Flags and how to identify if you might be seeing one unfold before your eyes.[66] Again, what he says has direct connection to conspiracy theories, because False Flags are in fact conspiracies and these in turn fuel conspiracy theories, for good reason! When you see the following list of things, your Spidey Sense should be tingling. The more things in the list you see, the more you should realize that the Green Goblin is probably right behind you.

---

[66] See especially Richard Dolan, *False Flags*, Episode 1, *Gaia* (2017).

- *A spectacular and emotional (traumatic) and unusual event.*
- *Instant media saturation.* All the national media instantly covers the event in the same way (often, local media differs). I don't know if you have ever seen one of those Brady Bunch side by side by side by side clips of 50 different news stations all saying exactly the same thing about the same event or not. If you haven't, it is worth looking up. If you have, you know exactly what this one is talking about.
- *The case is quickly closed.* Real investigations are messy, but in false flags, in one day, the official story is delivered. Case closed. Furthermore, the media refuses to question the official narrative.
- *A convenient patsy or scapegoat.* Lee Harvey Oswald. Timothy McVeigh. The Jews. The Pols. Stalin's fictious reactionaries. White supremists, Muslims—people need a bad guy. Is there one almost immediately shown to the world?
- *Decisive and negative government action.* This is the whole point of false flag. It is always supported by the media machine. Very few question the action. This is often all the more alarming because from what you will hear them say at other times, this is precisely the action they say they stand against. Further, these actions:
    - Further erode citizen's rights, usually in the name of safety and protection. The actions lead to increasing police or regulatory power by the state.
    - Often leads to an invasion or regime change of another country that could never otherwise be justified.
- *Anomalies and questions arise.* Discrepancies. This is what we have seen naturally happens when any conspiracy is taking place. We live in a republic and we need a free press and, these days, a free internet (good luck with both) so that people can do the hard work of real investigation, such as the independent work of "The Citizens Commission to Investigate the FBI" where several "burglars" in the media broke into a small FBI office and stole all the files which led to the fall of Nixon.
- Finally, ask yourself who benefits from what is taking place before my eyes.

Importantly, you aren't to be looking for just one of these things and if you see it declare that you have found the silver bullet and that the thing must be a false flag, hence conspiracy. In fact, that's the opposite thing you should be doing, for this is exactly what gives conspiratorial thinking such a bad rep. It's like saying that a half-truth is the whole truth. These are tell-tale signs that accompany known false flags, and thus real conspiracies. The more you can obviously see, the more suspicious you should be. If there's only one or two, it's a good bet you either haven't dug deep enough or it really is exactly what it appears to be.

The Myth of Neutrality

Something to be very leery of are claims of neutrality. In journalism, objectivity is an ideal that the reporter is supposed to be aiming for. Objectivity allows a person to get outside of their own bias in order to think clearly about the facts. Remember Joe Friday from Dragnet? "Just the facts, ma'am." It is possible to report on a story in an objective manner, without showing much bias. Obviously, the less personally involved one is on the subject, the easier that is to do.

But a lot of people confuse objectivity with *neutrality*. Neutrality is a prior condition to objectivity. Neutrality means that a person comes to a story without any bias whatsoever. Again, there are plenty of stories that a person doesn't care about one way or the other that allows their objectivity to be more easily gained. But I believe on most things a person can be objective without first being neutral. Ironically, it is only possible if the person first admits that they are in fact not neutral. That way, they admit their own bias to themselves and others and this makes it possible to begin to look at honestly. It is when someone is not in fact neutral and will not admit that they are biased that causes their investigation to be anything but objective.

A radio talk-show host in Denver used to always say, "Tell

me where you sit before you tell me where you stand." In other words, before the caller began to make his argument (usually against the host's view), he wanted to know what his biases were. Doing this makes it much easier to spot when a person is hiding something or has a secret agenda they aren't telling you about. I've noticed over the years that most conservative hosts openly admit that they are conservative, while far fewer hosts on the left ever admit their own bias. For whatever reason, many on the left somehow think that they are in fact "in the middle." They pretend neutrality, like they are the pristine island of "the middle." This puts their ability to actually be objective in great danger, especially if it is something they actually care about.

There are several versions of a chart on media bias that are floating around the internet right now. It's like a flow chart of who is conservative and who is liberal (i.e. leftist) and who is neutral. What's hysterical to me about all of those versions is how everyone single one of the media conglomerates that we know for a fact were in bed with the CIA in operation Mockingbird are always presented as neutral (NBC, CBS, Washington Post, New York Times, etc.). It's a joke. Any thinking person ought to be able to see through this. Sadly, many can't.

Understanding that no one is perfectly neutral and that we all have biases is a good place to start. And that is nothing to be ashamed of, either. If you hold a view, be proud of it. Tell others about it. Then, if you are trying to think through two sides of an issue, set it aside for a moment, try to take the other side seriously, try to understand what it is saying, and learn to be objective. This is what we used to teach when we taught children logic and rhetoric in school. This is what journalism is supposed to be teaching media professionals. Those tools are more valuable and needed today than ever before.

With all this said, as you are considering the things you are hearing, look for coherence, check out facts, see if those line up with reality. Watch out for circular reasoning. Think about if what you are hearing is absolutely and forever something that will be impossible to verify or falsify. Learn signs of what to look out for when being sold a story. Be aware of journalistic spin. Remember that people often have agendas, especially very large billion-dollar corporations! Always beware of your own biases and predispositions towards wanting a thing to be true or false. Don't engage in your own kind of propaganda or astroturfing when talking about a subject to others. Remain calm and rational. Take the high road in your interactions with those who disagree with you. Learn to think critically about the things you are hearing and seeing. Don't just take someone's word for it, especially in these dark days. As the Apostle Paul said, "Test everything" (1Th 5:21) If you will heed these few tips, the world of conspiracy theories will be a much safer place for you.

SUPPLEMENT TO
REPORT NO.

THIS IS UNEVALUATED INFORMATION

REMAINING SANE IN A WORLD OF CONSPIRACIES

CONFIDENTIAL

REGRADED SECRET
Authority NND 750065
By EB/OT, NARS, Date MARCH 15, 1976
SECRET WRITING

EXEMPT from automatic declassification
per E.O. 11052, Sec. 5(E)(2)
TURNER cia 28 JAN 1978
Name   Agency   Date
A   2020
Reason   Review on
E.78-4 par

Movie or Real Life?

JERRY FLETCHER IS THE TAXICAB driver in the movie *Conspiracy Theory* who just won't shut up. No matter who gets into his cab, Jerry has a story to tell them … about conspiracy theories. Jerry knows every conspiracy theory there ever was, and his life of total paranoia proves it. For years, maybe decades, Jerry has thought that the government is out to get him! He can't even walk into his apartment building through the front door but has to scale the roof and then descend down several flights of stairs so no one will see where he lives. He has several deadbolt locks on his doors, and his apartment is rigged to blow at a moment's notice, to destroy all evidence of all the conspiracies that he had accumulated throughout the years.

I won't ruin the story for you if you haven't seen the movie, but the beginning, where this view of Jerry is presented to us, is one of the main reasons I've written this book, and especially why I've written it at this moment. Conspiracy theories can have real consequences upon people's lives. This is all the truer right now when so many people (whether they admit it to themselves of not) are entertaining them. Before looking into those consequences, let's explore for a moment some of the reasons this is happening in order to drive home to the point that this topic and the real-life consequences it can have is vital to begin talking about publicly.

Current Events

This strange snapshot in world history that I find myself writing in—the coronavirus pandemic of 2020—has people scared. There is this deep collective anxiety all around us because no one knows what will emerge on the other side of this contagion. The world is holding its collective breath. When they let it out will it be a sigh or a scream? I heard just from someone that they know a woman who died this week simply from the stress. I saw another post of a man who committed suicide because he couldn't take the social distancing. I keep getting questions about the End of Days. When people get scared, they look for explanations of events that will calm them and bring them some iota of internal peace. Many people think that conspiracy theories can help them manage the unknown. To some degree this is true; to another degree it isn't.

Technological Catalysts

As I have unfolded for you in the previous chapters, conspiracy theories are everywhere. As you've seen, I haven't been able to get away from them. My friends can't get away from them. My family can't. This world can't. They have become ubiquitous. Your neighbor is entertaining them, your uncle, your niece, your congressmen, your boss, and your pastor. Yes, even your pastor, he just won't tell you. This one goes out to all my fellow pastors who have pictures of bigfoot on the walls *of your minds*. You know who you are.

Part of this is just the world that we live in. The technologies that we have invented lend themselves perfectly to them. Nearly infinite numbers of websites giving every possible view of any given event; social media where everyone can and does say just about anything they want to say about everything; 24-hour "news" on several cable channels ... These are not going away any time soon. All of this and so much more lends itself to the spreading of ideas like virus' spread through a body.

In the fascinating movie *Inception*, the main character Cobb asks a question relevant to this moment in time. "What's the most resilient parasite? A bacteria? A virus? An intestinal worm? An idea. Resilient, highly contagious. Once an idea's taken hold in the brain, it's almost impossible to eradicate." Later he concludes, "Resilient ... highly contagious, and an idea can grow. The smallest seed of an idea can grow to define or destroy your world." How about "the" world? What's ironic about this movie citation is that it is itself a movie about a kind of conspiracy theory, making it work on a double-level both of the immediate context of the words of the quotation and on the deeper level of the context of the conspiracy to implant ideas in people's minds without their knowledge or consent.

The American and World Experiment

We've seen how conspiracy theories are part and parcel of what it has always meant to be American (and probably many more nationalities as well). Our national identity has been shaped since the very beginning by conspiracy theories. Many of these have been true theories. Yes, there are many true conspiracy theories; they are not all "myths," "fables," and wild speculations of the imagination. Remember, for most of our history, this kind of thinking wasn't viewed as taboo at all. In fact, it was quite acceptable, even expected!

Throughout history, conspiracies and arising counter-theories have been part of every culture. They are even found in the Bible. Some have brought much confusion and hurt to many people. Some have obscured the truth of some pretty important things, even being an instrumental cause in some people rejecting Jesus Christ as the King of king! Some have brought to light true conspiracies, such as what we find in Psalm 2. These are just a few of the consequences that can come from conspiracy theories.

I wish that we could return to the day when some degree of conspiratorial thinking was viewed as normal and healthy, because all this means is that people are actually thinking for themselves rather than feeding their faces with whatever propaganda they hear on cable news. But those days are gone. And with them, so also a healthy understanding of how they can be both good and bad for people.

Demonization of the Phrase

In recent years, we have seen that there has been a known and concerted effort to stigmatize and demonize "conspiracy theory" as an idea, as that which belongs only to the realm of kooks and nut-jobs. Who wants to be associated with that? This has created only more confusion, hurt only more people, and brought about what I think is becoming a kind of crisis for many, perhaps even for our civilization itself.

I also think that part of the explosion of underground conspiratorial thinking is being brought on by the power of the forbidden. If it is demonized, some are attracted to it because they are told that they are not supposed to engage in it. Like the proverbial cookie jar that is off limits to a child, its only purpose is to make him obsess over what is inside. I also believe that the explosion of hatred that has erupted in the last couple of years in this country is being exacerbated by this demonization and how, because of it, our culture refuses to talk about this subject or to take it seriously.

A Free Press?

The hatred is also fueled by how politically charged the subject is and how it is supposedly only one side that engages in conspiratorial thinking. Most of this is coming to us from a press that feigns neutrality (see previous chapter), yet is anything but. We have seen the direct CIA involvement in the mainstream media and how reporters even tell us to our faces that it is their job to tell us what to think. But there is more.

For example, most people do not realize that in 2020, 90% of all media in the United States is owned by just four media conglomerates (Comcast [via NBCUniversal]), Disney, ViacomCBS (controlled by National Amusements), and AT&T (via Warner-Media). This is a radical, almost impossible to fathom change from just a few decades ago. As recently as 1984, fifty independent media companies own the majority of media. In radio, since 1996, Clear Channel Communications grew from 40 stations to 1200, in all 50 states. That's one corporation that owns 1200 radio stations. Think of it. Think of the power over our minds that they could had be if they so wanted it. Quite bluntly, I believe they do want it. There is a reason why station after station gives the exact same story with the exact same wording and spin. There are reasons that when ratings fall networks only double-down on their insanely biased coverage. It isn't about money anymore. It is about control and power over people.

Furthermore, consider the words of former CBS correspondent Lara Logan,

The media everywhere is mostly liberal. Not just in the U.S. But in this country, 85 percent of journalists are registered Democrats. So that's just a fact, right? ... So the facts are on the side of what you just stated. Most journalists are left or liberal or Democrat or whatever word you want to give it. I always joke about the other 14 percent were too lazy to register. And there's maybe one percent that's on the right. There's one Fox. And there's many, many many more organizations on the left ... Both sides do terrible things. Both sides lie. Both sides manipulate. Both sides push their point of view. But the problem is the weight of all of these organizations on one side of the political spectrum. When you turn on your computer or you walk past the TV or you see a newspaper headline in the grocery store, if they are all saying the same thing, the weight of that convinces you that it's true. You don't question it because everyone is saying it.[67]

Logan is no conservative,[68] but she has integrity and realizes that the state of the media today is little more than a propaganda machine for the Democratic Party and its special interests. This is made clear when you understand things like how during the recent impeachment hearings, literally almost 100% of news coverage of the story was negative towards the sitting president.[69] This is not objective journalism by any definition of the word. It can't help but spawn conspiracy theories, and the damage it is causing to the country is incalculable. It is, quite literally, causing people to hate one another. Do yourself a favor and turn off the news.

[67] Tim Hains, "Lara Logan Slams Media For Becoming Left-Wing 'Propagandists' With "Horse—" Low Standards," *RealClear* (Feb 19, 2019), https://www.realclearpolitics.com/video/2019/02/19/lara_logan_hits_media_for_becoming_left-wing_propagandists_horseshit_low_standards.html
[68] Joe Concha, "Lara Logan: 'I'm Not Going to Pretend to be Conservative' to be Conservative Media 'Darling,'" *The Hill* (Feb 26, 2019), https://thehill.com/homenews/media/431561-lara-logan-im-not-going-to-pretend-to-be-conservative-to-be-conservative-media.
[69] Matt Palumbo, "Media's Trump Coverage Now 100% Negative During Impeachment Hysteria," *The Dan Bongino Show* (Jan 30, 2020), https://bongino.com/medias-trump-coverage-now-100-negative-during-impeachment-hysteria/.

Explosion of Immorality

Closely related to this is a world gone crazy with immorality, greed, power, money, and control. The constant promotion and glorification of biblically rebellious lifestyles and the constant demonization of morality by the press and their cohorts in crime in other forms of mass communication (especially higher education and Hollywood) are greatly to blame. And again, the more out of control those things get, the more conspiracies there will be, and the more confusing the world around us will appear.

So, we have a crisis on our hands. It is a crisis of conspiracy theories in the worst possible sense of that phrase. But this crisis is creating even a greater crisis, one that Jerry Fletcher demonstrates perfectly in the movie. It is a crisis of the human soul. Jerry shows through a movie how important this question is to deal with properly. My own experience, both personal and anectodical confirms it. So, in the remainder of this chapter I want to ask, *how can a Christian remain sane* in a world of conspiracy theories?

Understand What *Conspiracy Theories* Can Do to You

Dangers

Perhaps the thing that has been on my mind the most while thinking about this book is trying to help those entangled in the complicated webs of conspiracy theories to understand what these things can do negatively to a mind and soul. How can conspiratorial thinking, that is, a kind of pattern of thought that becomes a way of life, negatively affect you? A lot of people think conspiracy theories can help them manage the unknown and as I said earlier, to some degree that might be true. But in the meantime, there are other costs to be had.

I've seen how getting really worked up about these things works itself out time and time again through emotions like worry, anxiety, fear, obsession, mistrust, anger, frustration, and a sense of helplessness.

- *Worry.* Some people are naturally prone to worry, which as our Lord Jesus teaches us, is a sin. Worry is a kind of unease that causes a mind to dwell upon the unknown, particularly the difficulties and troubles of life. Depending upon the conspiracy theory, worry can be greatly exacerbated simply by the content of the theory. For example, a conspiracy theory that sees the illuminati and other global elites doing all in their power to create a one world government where they will force all Christians to take the mark of the beast or die, could probably create a bit of worry (to say the least).
- *Anxiety.* Closely associated with worry is anxiety. Anxiety is nervousness and unease about imminent events that have an uncertain outcome. For example, if you believed in a conspiracy theory where aliens were watching your house and were taking you each night to probe you in their spaceship, you would probably be a rather anxious person. Just like worry, anxiety is not an emotion that demonstrates faith in Christ.
- *Fear.* Perhaps the end of worry and anxiety is fear. Fear is caused when you think something dangerous is likely to cause pain or worse. In the alien conspiracy theory above, imagine if you believed aliens were tearing your limbs off only to reattach them to the body before returning you to earth? That would be terrifying. In fact, there are many people who suffer with this exact fear right now.
- *Obsession.* Obsession is when a thought or idea perpetually invades the mind so that a person is constantly preoccupied with that thought. This is a very clear and present danger of many conspiracies, and the wilder the theory, the more prone people are to obsess over it. Obsession is dangerous because it crowds out all other thoughts, including those we need to recover from the very dangers presented in this list. Right now, a lot of people are absolutely obsessed with Q. They read hours and hours of twitter posts, watch scores of Q related videos, spend all their time trying to work out all the riddles and paradoxes. For some, there is little else worth thinking about or doing in their life. This is obsession and it is extremely detrimental to the well-being of both body and soul.

- *Mistrust.* Mistrust is when a person is suspicious of someone else. This is a curious one, because in the hatred spoken above going on in our culture right now between conservatives and leftists, there is a great deal of mistrust to be had, especially when we put a famous person's picture associated with the opposite view as mine into our spotlight. Trust is something that is earned and many people, we think, have not earned our trust. That's perfectly reasonable. But when such mistrust is so broadly stroked that it becomes a stereotype of all in the group, this becomes bigotry and, quite honestly, its source is a conspiracy theory. This is one of the reasons I believe both sides of this cultural divide are engaging in conspiratorial thinking, even though in my experience it is usually just the one side (the conservatives) that gets blamed for it. There is nothing that can tear apart the fabric of unity and brotherhood than mistrust. While there are several things in this list that make me think of him, mistrust (or paranoia) is a vice that someone like Alex Jones from *InfoWars* exudes. The deeper into conspiracy theories he has gotten over the years, the worse this has become. When you hear someone constantly spouting off that there is danger around every corner, that people are always out to get them, that they have sources but can't tell anyone who they are, or who suggest that those who mock or try to disprove them are really on the other team, mistrust and paranoia are close by. Beware.
- *Anger.* Anger is a strong feeling of annoyance, displeasure, or hostility. It is easily associated with conspiratorial thinking. Again, think of Jones. The man flies off the handle almost every episode. He is not calm, but a profoundly angry person. Or consider a particular conspiracy theory. Imagine if you thought that the purpose of the coronavirus was really that the government could secretly install 5g towers all over the world in a devious plot to control the minds of all humans on earth. This could make you very angry. In fact, we have seen this past week in several countries, people violently tearing down 5g towers for just this reason. What happens when that anger reaches a boiling point and it is people rather than towers that the rage turns against?
- *Frustration.* Frustration is when that annoyance is turned inward rather than outward. It occurs because the person has this

impending doom that there is no chance of changing the trajectory. As I speak, a growing sense of frustration is occurring among Q followers, because it feels like time is running out for the theory to be true. Yet, it is accompanied by a tremendous feeling that the underlying evils of human trafficking, satanic ritual abuse, cannibalism, and elites who are using these things to summon spiritual powers to their aid is all too real. If that doesn't change, it would give anyone a sense of pent up frustration.

- *Helplessness*. Helplessness is when the frustration reaches in inward driven boiling point. Helplessness is the inability to defend oneself or to act effectively for others. Take the previous illustration. This week I watched a young woman give an interview of having come out of that very situation. She was used for sex and rituals her entire childhood life. She has a clear sense of helplessness in that video and it certainly spread to me when I watched it.

Solutions

Each of these are unhealthy states of the mind that are often linked directly to sin. How is a Christian to deal with them? Here are some things I think are helpful. The first and most important thing is that you must have and/or continue having faith in Christ. What does this mean? Hebrews 11:1 tells us, "Faith is the assurance of things hoped for, the conviction of things not seen."

Many people think that faith is some kind of blind leap in the dark rooted in wishful thinking. This is not a biblical view of faith. Faith is an assurance of things hoped for. Specifically, he is talking about our future eternal state—the resurrection of our bodies and eternal life with God in the new heavens and earth. But on what basis should anyone have such an assured hope?

On the basis *of the past*. Christianity is unlike all other religions in this regard. The things "not seen," certainly include God the Father in heaven who has made all things through is Word, for this is the very next thing Hebrews tells us (Heb 11:3). But it also includes God's work in this world in the past through the

Son of God in the Old Testament. Here I'm talking about how people both knew and worshiped the Son of God in those days gone by. When it says Abraham believed God and it was credited to him as righteousness (Gen 15:6), it is speaking about the God he was looking at, the God he "saw" (Gen 15:1). This is the Son of God—The Angel of the LORD. It does not say Abraham believed in something in the future; it says he believed God. The Son spoke to Abraham and he believed him. Many people in Israel never got to see the Son (that is the Angel of the LORD), but they still believed in him. Why?

They had evidence. The KJV translates "the conviction of things not seen" as "evidence." Evidence is demonstrable proof that something is real. It is the opposite of a leap in the dark. When God lead his people out of Egypt with a mighty hand, he gave them evidence: ten plagues, a miraculous sea-parting, water from a rock in the dessert, manna from heaven. He proved himself to them.

There is much evidence for God throughout the Scripture, for it never asks us to believe in him apart from evidence. But the greatest evidence, and thus the greatest hope for things unseen is the coming of Jesus Christ in human flesh. In his time with us, as one of us, Jesus performed many miracles, including predicting very specific things about his own death and resurrection. Then, he proved them true by rising from the dead and being seen by many witnesses in his glorified state. They saw him. They talked with him. They ate with him. They even touched him. In other words, our hope for things future rests entirely upon the truth of things past—things that have come to pass in Jesus Christ.

This Jesus is called at his birth the king. During his ministry he is the king. At the cross he is the king. In his resurrection he is the king. At his ascension he is the King of kings. This King is omnipotent, meaning that he along with his Father and the Holy Spirit are all powerful. They can do anything they want in heaven or on earth. Not only can they; they in fact do anything they want in heaven and on earth. This is proven to you by the impossible— raising Jesus from the dead.

Faith places trust that Jesus is in fact the King of kings, more, than he is God of gods. It believes him when he says these things about himself. This simple faith is what justifies a person in God's eyes, so that whatever sins they have committed are forgiven by the only one who is able to forgive sins—God alone.

But this faith also continues throughout our lives. When we worry, are anxious, and begin to fear, we have faith that God is in control and that Jesus has all things in his hand. His is absolutely sovereign over the affairs of the entire universe. There is not even a single maverick molecule to be found. What then can the worst conspiracy to do to him or his plan?

When we have mistrust in others and become angry, we re- member that God is wholly trustworthy and has proven it by making us new creatures in Christ by faith alone because of his grace alone. When we become frustrated and begin to feel help- less, we remember that this God is omnipotent and nothing thwarts his will.

Faith is an outward looking. It is a taking our eyes off of our- selves. That means it is also a taking our eyes off of the conspiracy theories. Looking outward and upward means you are no longer looking inward or downward or horizontally at the world. In my estimation, this is the only lasting solution to the traps that con- spiracy theories can put us in. Yes, many non-Christians are able to avoid these traps; but our goal is not merely to avoid traps, it is to be saved from the trap of sin itself. And only Christ Jesus can rescue a person from this.

I want you to assume for the sake of argument that every conspiracy theory I just gave above corresponds to reality (see be- low). In other words, they are true. Should that impact at all how a Christian should respond to them? My answer is, no. It shouldn't. Why? Because the same solutions I gave are true whether the theory itself is true or false. Our minds are quite subjective things, and whether a theory is actually true does not often matter in terms of what it is able to do to our minds and souls.

No matter how sound a theory is and no matter how dire or terrible is may be, God is always on his Throne and nothing can take him off of it. Not evil people. Not extra-terrestrials. Not angels or demons. Not Hillary Clinton or Donald Trump. Not Q and not you! Therefore, the first solution to these traps is to rest in the finished work of Jesus Christ on the cross. His death was a substitution that you might be forgiven. His resurrection was the firstfruits of a harvest that you too might have life. Look to Christ and sins will begin to melt away.

A second thing to talk about here is the work of the Holy Spirit in a person's life. Jesus ascended to heaven so that he might send the Holy Spirit to live in the lives of each and every Christian. Jesus could not do that, because he was embodied as a man. But through his Spirit, he can do it, for Spirit is something immaterial.

The Holy Spirit of God is not a force, not a thing. He is a person. He is the Third Person of the Holy Trinity, equal in being and nature to the Father and Son in every possible way. They are One. One of the things the Holy Spirit does in a Christian's life is produce fruit. Listen to the fruit of the Spirit. "But the fruit of the Spirit is love, joy, peace, patience, kindness, goodness, faithfulness, gentleness, self-control; against such things there is no law" (Gal 5:22-23). Now compare this with my previous list: worry, anxiety, fear, obsession, mistrust, anger, frustration, and helplessness.

Do these things sound the same? Of course not. They are opposites. One group comes from God; the other comes from a God-complex. I'm guessing many have not thought of those that way. What is worry, anxiety, and fear, what are frustration and helplessness if not feelings that arise because we believe we should be able do something about the future, about the impossible, about the unknowable? That's a God-complex. It is taking the attributes that only God has and superimposing them upon ourselves. Perhaps that's a strange thing to think about, a new thought to you. If it is true, what is the solution? It can't be to turn inward upon yourself, but to turn outward to the only One who is God and to beg forgiveness.

If you know yourself to be caught in a cycle of conspiratorial thinking and feel you can't get out and know it is causing these negative things in your soul, pray to God, turn from these things, and begin meditating on the fruit of the Spirit. Read the Psalms. Deliberate on the things of God from what is truly the other-world. Think on his salvation. Contemplate his absolute forgiveness of all of your sins. Put your mind on things above. Put down the conspiracy books; shut down the websites, take a break from the media (actually, never watch the media!). God will begin filling you up with fruit that others will want to eat too.

Finally, I have what you might think is a rather strange application for such obsession. Have fun! For some people, conspiracy thinking is a deadly serious business. That's Jerry Fletcher. For me, the world of conspiracies is fascinating, interesting, and, quite frankly, fun. That doesn't mean that *the conspiracies* are fun. Many of them are anything but. It does mean the idea itself is fun. If God is really on his throne, then we do not have to be so serious about these things, no matter how earth shattering they claim to be. He knows what he is doing, and he knows what is really going on. As we research and keep this in mind, it can make hard things much easier to swallow (especially if they happen to be true). God gives us this life to enjoy life. I think a person can have fun in this field and still enjoy life, even enjoying the process of learning about conspiracy theories. But only if they are a means to an end.

One of the things that is fun for me about them is thinking

about you and others while doing it. Specifically, if I can use my strange hobby to help others, especially to help them come to know Christ or to walk a godlier life, then that makes it fun! I'm having fun writing this book, hopefully making it enjoyable with a little levity sprinkled in to lighten such a serious subject. It's because I want people to read it and have fun and to learn and hopefully even to grow in Christ. Because they are not an end to themselves, it makes thinking about conspiracies more interesting to me because I'm using them to think about how knowing this information might be able to help someone else. You see? The goal here is not knowing and worrying and obsessing on the theory, but on using it as a tool to glorify God through it. And yes, I very much think that this subject can be used to glorify God, not by ignoring it, but by bringing it to the light of day and shining the truth of Christ upon it.

Understand What *Conspiracies* Can Do to You

Dangers

Look carefully at the difference in the heading of this section compared to the last. Previously, I dealt with what *conspiracy theories* can do to you. Here, I'm looking at the opposite—what real *conspiracies* can do you to whether you have a theory about it or not. This is the world of true evil where dark and shady deals are made in secret places to the harm of someone else, usually on some kind of important level that will end up impacting a lot of people, including you.

If I'm concerned with how easy it is to get wrapped up and consumed by conspiracy theories and how people might not even recognize what is happening to them, I am almost as concerned about those who refuse to entertain the idea of conspiracies at all. Here I'm not talking about the person who simply doesn't care about conspiracies. To each his own. I'm talking about the person who gets angry about the thought of a conspiracy theory. I've met plenty of these kinds of people. They'll curse you out to your face for even daring to bring it up. We've seen how this phrase is used very disparagingly towards others, as a put down, as a thought-stopper, as a way of hurting someone who is entertaining an idea rather than engaging them where they are.[70]

---

[70] A classic example of this appeared this week in *Christianity Today*. See Ed Stetzer, "On Christians Spreading Corona Conspiracies: Gullibility is not a Spiritual Gift," *Christianity Today* (April 15, 2020),
https://www.christianitytoday.com/edstetzer/2020/april/christians-and-corona-conspiracies.html?fbclid=IwAR0fB_Y2150JqraOl8Z_ZidnXeUdfZuo3MQxnMZ Q92HRoo6FitOCV2C1NL0; also Ed Stetzer, "Christians, Repent (Yes, Repent) of Spreading Conspiracy Theories and Fake News—It's Bearing False Witness," *Christianity Today* (May 31, 2017),
https://www.christianitytoday.com/edstetzer/2017/may/christians-repent-conspiracy-theory-fake-news.html.

In these articles, Stetzer assumes our CIA definition of "conspiracy theory" as something that is "speculation on hidden meanings" or gossipy "juicy secrets," rather than responsible, reasonable alternative theories based in solid evidence (the older definition). He begs questions all over the place essentially saying you should just trust whatever the official story is, because conspiracy theories are "unfounded." "You need to go to trusted sources," he says, not those who "peddle in conspiracy theories." What are those exactly? He never says. He resorts of *ad hominem* by calling those who dare to dabble in this field "foolish," "fake news," "peddlers," "hate-driven," "silly," "gullible," "stupid," necessary violators of the eighth commandment (in other words, liars), and "sinners." The best one is when he mockingly says, "If you still insist on [spreading these], would you please consider taking Christian off your bio so the rest of us don't have to share in the embarrassment you are heaping on yourself." Besides the fact that he says Christians are supposed to be fueled by love, I sense little in that statement or pretty much in the sum of the two pieces. They just mock and ridicule and shut down all thought.

He makes some valid points, such as it is true that there are some plain old evil conspiracy theories out there that are only meant to hurt people or like how there are scammers who create these just to dupe people (both of those are actually fairly deep subjects on their own). But he does it while poo-pooing theories that in fact have never been proven false (like pizzagate, maybe he should talk to investigative journalist Liz Crokin about that one). He never gives any evidence whatsoever, other than his own word, that we should believe what he is saying, like he's the expert and we should just trust him. Most of all, he shuts down all opposition with his inflammatory language. His articles are not there to help, but to stop all critical thinking about this important topic in its tracks. He is exactly the kind of person I'm talking to in this section.

To this group I first want to say, do you seriously not think that you are not also entertaining one conspiracy theory or another without knowing it? Do you really think you are immune? Is it even possible that someone could intentionally be deceiving you, and how would you even know if you aren't willing to even entertain the idea? Do you believe that absolutely everything you hear an "authority" tell you and that you presently hold true is absolute truth? It isn't possible that you could be wrong? In my mind, that is just as much a God-complex as what we just spoke about. You are not more omniscient than the former group is omnipotent.

Furthermore, if there is one thing many conspiracies have in common, it is that people are not basically good. I will have more to say about this in the last section. For now, one of the fundamental truths of the Bible is that people are sinful, through and through. To take a view that all conspiracy theories are evil is to presuppose that those telling you what reality looks like are basically good, always have your best interest at heart, and would never lie to you about anything.

Here, I'm painting with a broad brush. I realize that. I'm not saying that everything you hear about everything is deceptive or intentionally misleading. Nor am I saying that even most people are like this most of the time. God's common grace is a remarkable thing. I'm saying that to constantly demean this subject is to ignore a broader reality of human evil. We've seen proof in this book that even our own government lies to us. Certainly, the media does. Sometimes it can be for good reasons, I suppose. Other times, not so much. To ignore this reality now that you have seen the truth is to live in a conspiracy theory of your own making, which is that the world is not really like this. That goes against the evidence. It goes against reality. And it goes against one's own belief that they do not entertain conspiracy theories. How deliciously ironic.

Again, it isn't that I particularly care if whole swaths of people never think about conspiracy theories. Not everyone has to or even should go down this road. What I care about is those who constantly use this phrase to stop the conversation and hurt other people. Because that's what it does. You may think that a certain conspiracy theory hurts other people. Great. Don't be a jerk about it. Talk civilly to them. Show respect for your fellow human being. People have no idea how many others there are out there considering alternative views of things. Trust me, they are thinking about them; they just won't tell you about it because it isn't safe to do so.

Probably the most important arena of life this occurs is with Christianity. I thoroughly believe Christianity is true. That's because it is true. But that doesn't stop conspiracy theories that go from the tallest ivory towers down to the lowliest ordinary person from rising up around it. And, honestly, that isn't a bad thing. Because if Christianity is true, it will stand up to the scrutiny.

The way to help someone entertaining a conspiracy theory against God and his Christ is not to shut them down. The solution is to engage them where they are. It can also be as helpful for you as them when you begin thinking about these things anew, putting on a new pair of glasses, and to beginning thinking about others before ourselves. In this way, we will do to others as we want them to do to us, which is the Golden Rule, after all.

Finally, I'm also going to tell you the same thing I told the previous group. Have fun! Life is too short to be cantankerous over this subject, or over anything, really. Consider the flat earth conspiracy which studies incredibly say that 1/3 of millennials think could be true.[71] I personally know several people who believe it. And the anger I see spewed in both directions on their social media platforms in astounding. What good does it do to get angry about it? It is what it is. So, learn a little bit about the view and engage people with reason that isn't so serious it

---

[71] "A Third of Millennials Aren't Sure The Earth Is Round, Survey Finds," *CBS Pittsburgh* (Apr 5, 2018), https://pittsburgh.cbslocal.com/2018/04/05/millennials-flat-earth-survey/.

thinks it is the end of the world if people have a wrong view of something. In these days of coronavirus, I think people might be getting a glimpse of the truth that life is too short for the first time in a long time, whether the conspiracy theories surrounding it are true or not.

Human Depravity and Conspiracy Theories

Something else is being revealed in all this. I spoke briefly about it a moment ago. I think these conflicts are exposing something about the human heart that demonstrates that people are not basically good. How they do this can differ from case to case. Sometimes they expose actual human evil that is being done to cover a thing up. Other times, they expose our own unwillingness to investigate the facts and to just believe whatever we are told. That isn't necessarily a bad thing, but it sure can be. Still other times, they expose a serious flaw in our nature which is to obsess about hidden things, like Jerry. This is most certainly not good, especially for Christians.

I truly wish I didn't have to go into detail on this overwhelmingly obvious doctrine of the Bible, especially when I believe most of my audience will be Christian. But we are not living in a day when the church is doing a whole lot to actually teach Christians what God's word says about pretty much anything. Put bluntly, I believe we are living in a new dark ages in the church of Jesus Christ, though I continue to pray he would wake pastors, teachers, and all Christians up to the fact that we are stammering around like drunken sailors wondering where the word of God is, but we can't find it.

Conspiracies, astroturfing, false flags, PSYOPs, infiltration, bias and spin, and other things we have addressed in this book reinforce the biblical position that human beings are not basically good. This seems self-evident to those who know what true conspiracies are like and the kinds of things their perpetrators will do. But even in the world of Q (as my continuing current living example), I constantly find those on the side of Q saying that if people will just wake up, we will finally discover that people are not really evil. It is just a few evil people who have, for whatever reasons, gone over to the Dark Side.

This is not only naïve, it is dangerous thinking. For it says that if I were the one in charge, I would not be prone to doing what *those* people are doing. I would stop it and replace their evil conspiracy with a utopia. Guess what? That's precisely what Lenin and Stalin believed. They were not the evil ones; those were the oligarchy, the elites, the bourgeois. They were immune to the things that deceived others and made them so evil. So, the communists would come to the rescue of the poor and working people and usher in the Second Coming.

Jordan Peterson has a great line about this, and for someone I would call at the present moment a "Nobel Pagan," he has an incredibly healthy view of human depravity. When wondering aloud about what people mean when they say, "Well, that wasn't real communism," in an attempt to justify their communist and socialist worldviews, Peterson replies,

> That's the most arrogant statement a person can possibly make. I know what that means. I've thought about it for years. It means I am so narcissistic and arrogant and so convinced of the rightness of my ideology and my moral purity, that if I was the dictator of the communist state, the utopia would have come in as promised. That's what it means.[72]

Here then is what all people entertaining conspiracy theories must come to grips with. It isn't just *"those people"* who are evil. *I* am evil. No one is "basically good." That's a pagan worldview. A biblical worldview is Romans 3, which is nothing but a litany of Old Testament passages strung together to make this overwhelming point.

---

[72] Peterson has said this many times. Here's one example. Jordan B. Peterson, "Jordan B Peterson Debunks the 'It Wasn't Real Communism' Argument," *YouTube* (Mar 5, 2017), https://www.youtube.com/watch?v=VsZJ0fJpLPc.

Both Jews and Greeks, are under sin, as it is written: "None is righteous, no, not one; no one understands; no one seeks for God. All have turned aside; together they have become worthless; no one does good, not even one" (Psalm 14:1-3; Ps 53:1-3). "Their throat is an open grave; they use their tongues to deceive" (Ps 5:9; Jer 5:16). "The venom of asps is under their lips" (Ps 140:3). "Their mouth is full of curses and bitterness" (Ps 10:7 LXX). "Their feet are swift to shed blood; in their paths are ruin and misery, and the way of peace they have not known" (Prov 1:15-17; Isa 59:7-8). "There is no fear of God before their eyes" (Ps 36:1).

This is not a pretty picture, nor is it meant to be. The whole point of this is to level every single human being to the same lowest possible playing field. We are all evil. Me and you. We all do bad things. In this specific regard, we are all committing conspiracy against God, defying him with our sinful rebellion as we saw in Psalm 2. Yes, some people make absolutely horrible choices that go beyond the normal sin, if you can call sin normal. Yes, there are some truly degenerate people in this world. And yes, many people do some very nice things. But Paul makes his point in the next verse. He is saying these things so that "the whole world may be held accountable to God" (Rom 3:19). Why?

Because this is the transition of the entire book of Romans. We understand that our good works are simply not good enough, no matter how good they are, and when we realize that we, like "they" have rebelled against God, then and only then does the good news make any sense to me.

The good news is not Q. It is not any other conspiracy theory, no matter how right it may be about a particular conspiracy of true evil. The good news is not that mankind will somehow overcome such and such an evil and usher in a utopia. The only utopia the world will ever know comes when Jesus returns in his Second Coming to judge the living and the dead, to separate the sheep from the goats, to wipe away every tear from those who called him king, and to remove the fullness of sins' penalty (already done), its power (ongoing in the life of a Christian), and its presence (the future we look forward to). Now the good news makes sense. And what is that news? The apostle continues,

> But now the righteousness of God has been manifested apart from the law, although the Law and the Prophets bear witness to it--the righteousness of God through faith in Jesus Christ for all who believe. For there is no distinction; for all have sinned and fall short of the glory of God, and are justified by his grace as a gift, through the redemption that is in Christ Jesus, whom God put forward as a propitiation by his blood, to be received by faith. This was to show God's righteousness, because in his divine forbearance he had passed over former sins. It was to show his righteousness at the present time, so that he might be just and the justifier of the one who has faith in Jesus.
> (Romans 3:21-26)

To be justified is to have God declare you "not guilty" before the court of heaven ... even though you *are* guilty. This "legal fiction" as some have blasphemously called it, is possible because God's righteousness was satisfied in the obedience of Christ who fully obeyed the law, perfect in every detail. It is possible because God's justice against lawbreakers was fully satisfied in the death of Christ, who did nothing deserving death, but underwent its punishment so that those who trust in him might have eternal life through union with him in resurrection. How? Because Scripture says those who are justified by faith in Christ become Christ's body with him as the Head. And if the Head is raised to eternal life, the body will be too.

The greatest conspiracy ever perpetrated was against this very same Jesus Christ and against his Father who sent him. It was a conspiracy committed by both seen and unseen enemies, those on earth and those in heavenly places. In sinning against this God, each of us is guilty in our own way of Christ's death, even as all the people of Jesus' own day—the Romans, the Jewish leaders, the people in Jerusalem, and even the disciples who all fled, were directly guilty of his crucifixion. "'The kings of the earth set themselves, and the rulers were gathered together, against the Lord and against his Anointed'—for truly in this city there were gathered together against your holy servant Jesus, whom you anointed, both Herod and Pontius Pilate, along with the Gentiles and the peoples of Israel, to do whatever your hand and your plan had predestined to take place" (Acts 4:26-28).

Those who reject that they have been part of that conspiracy are rejecting the only grace that can forgive them of their part in it. For his death was for your sin, that through faith you might be forgiven. How can anyone truly ever be sane in a world of conspiracy theories when they themselves remain guilty for their part in the Great Conspiracy that they have committed against God and his Christ?

Moreover, remember that I prefaced this chapter as a battle for souls. The battle for the soul cannot be fought with physical weapons, but only spiritual ones. The difficulty with so many true conspiracies is how devious, deceptive, and demonic they truly are. Even when we are not the main object of the conspiracy, their effects, both from the conspiracy itself that some don't even seem to care about and from the conspiracy theories that spring up around them, have this insidious pernicious ability to worm their way into your soul and begin gnawing away at its very fabric. The only way you can fight such a battle and win is if the living Christ and the Holy Spirit's armor are protecting you.

That armor makes you able to withstand in the evil day (Eph 6:13). It consists of truth. Truth is not something to be fled from but to be pursued. Always. Even if it is covered by a conspiracy theory. The truth *will* set you free. It contains your belt which holds your pants up so that you are not exposed to the world as a fool. It consists of righteousness—the fruit of the Spirit we talked about above. This is your breastplate which protects your heart. It is the shoes of the gospel, which makes you ready to give the good news to anyone who asks. It is faith, which shields you from the fiery darts of the devil. It is salvation, a helmet that protects your mind from irrational and wicked thoughts. It is the sword of the Holy Spirit, the Word of God, which is prayer and fellowship with the God who keeps you sane.

This is the perfect way to end a Christian look at conspiracy theories and all the things associated with them. I have discovered that as much as I love thinking about these strange things, the only thing that keeps me sane is knowing that I am forgiven of my own conspiracies I commit daily against the Living God. They may seem small to me, nothing compared to human trafficking, child-sacrificing, baby-cannibalizing Molech worshipers. But to God, those sins are as forgivable through the death of Christ as my sins are damnable apart from it.

Because I have come to know this forgiveness and this joy that the Holy Spirit has put into this Christian, I have come to see that people can in fact think well and, hopefully, properly about this taboo subject. They can even think Christianly about it. It is a worth-while pursuit to understand the world—the real world—around you. Neo learned that in the Matrix, didn't he? It is an honorable thing to want to uncover injustice and wicked-ness being perpetrated all around you. But what truly makes it worth-while, for me, is knowing that even in this rather strange hobby that I have, I know that God can be glorified through it. And since his glory will cover the earth as the waters cover the sea, if I can be of some small part in spreading the knowledge of him in order to help people who, like me, want to know truth, then I can sleep well at night.

I hope you have found something, hopefully a few things, in this book that made the read worthwhile.

With that said, there's really only one thing left for me to do.

I really want to watch the X-Files all over again now...

Greek

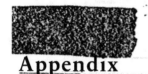

Appendix

SUPPLEMENT TO
REPORT NO.

THIS IS UNEVALUATED INFORMATION

CONCERNING CRITICISM OF THE WARREN REPORT

CONFIDENTIAL

REGRADED ~~SECRET~~
Authority NND 750065
By CR/97, RARS, Date MARCH 15, 1976

SECRET WRITING

EXEMPT from automatic declassification
per E.O. 11652, Sec. 5(E) (2)
Turner   CSR   28 JAN 1977
Name   Agency   Date
                  2020
Renewal   Review on
C.75-4 pgt:

This appendix shows copies of the CIA Document 1035-960 discussed in Chapter 2, along with a printed transcript courtesy of the website: JFK Lancer.[73]

---

[73] "CIA Document 1035-960: Concerning Criticism of the Warren Report," (April, 1967), http://www.jfklancer.com/CIA.html.

DISPATCH

	CLASSIFICATION	PROCESSING ACTION
	S E C R E T	MARKED FOR INDEXING

TO   Chiefs, Certain Stations and Bases

INFO.

Document Number 1035-960

X   NO INDEXING REQUIRED

ONLY QUALIFIED DESK CAN JUDGE INDEXING

FROM   Chief, WOVIEW

for FOIA Review on SEP 1976

CIA HISTORICAL REVIEW PROGRAM
Release in Full 1998

SUBJECT   Countering Criticism of the Warren Report

ACTION REQUIRED - REFERENCES

THIS WAS PULLED TOGETHER By NED BENNETT OF CA STAFF
PAUL H. FOR OSWALD   *IN CLOSE CONJUNCTION WITH CI/R&A: WE SUPPLIED MOST*
PSYCH   FILE + *OF THE SOURCE MATERIAL, PROVIDED MANY OF THE THEMES,*
         COPIES   *AND PROVIDED GENERAL "EXPERTISE" ON THE CASE. THE*   G.S. SOUTH
                   SEPTEMBER ARTICLE WAS WRITTEN BY BENNETT.   29 JAN
                                                                   196

1. Our Concern. From the day of President Kennedy's assassination on,
there has been speculation about the responsibility for his murder. Although
this was stemmed for a time by the Warren Commission report (which appeared at
the end of September 1964), various writers have now had time to scan the
Commission's published report and documents for new pretexts for questioning,
and there has been a new wave of books and articles criticizing the Commission's
findings. In most cases the critics have speculated as to the existence of some
kind of conspiracy, and often they have implied that the Commission itself was
involved. Presumably as a result of the increasing challenge to the Warren
Commission's Report, a public opinion poll recently indicated that 46% of the
American public did not think that Oswald acted alone, while more than half of
those polled thought that the Commission had left some questions unresolved.
Doubtless polls abroad would show similar, or possibly more adverse, results.

2. This trend of opinion is a matter of concern to the U.S. government,
including our organization. The members of the Warren Commission were naturally
chosen for their integrity, experience, and prominence. They represented both
major parties, and they and their staff were deliberately drawn from all sections
of the country. Just because of the standing of the Commissioners, efforts to
impugn their rectitude and wisdom tend to cast doubt on the whole leadership of
American society. Moreover, there seems to be an increasing tendency to hint
that President Johnson himself, as the one person who might be said to have
benefited, was in some way responsible for the assassination. Innuendo of
such seriousness affects not only the individual concerned, but also the whole
reputation of the American government. Our organization itself is directly
involved: among other facts, we contributed information to the investigation.
Conspiracy theories have frequently thrown suspicion on our organization, for
example by falsely alleging that Lee Harvey Oswald worked for us. The aim of
this dispatch is to provide material for countering and discrediting the claims
of the conspiracy theorists, so as to inhibit the circulation of such claims in
other countries. Background information is supplied in a classified section and
in a number of unclassified attachments.

3. Action. We do not recommend that discussion of the assassination question be initiated where it is not already taking place. Where discussion is
active, however, addressees are requested:

CS COPY.   201-289248

CROSS REFERENCE TO ABSTRACT	X	INDEX	DISPATCH SYMBOL AND NUMBER	DATE
9 attachments h/w			BD 5847	4/1/67
1 - SECRET *8 att.*			CLASSIFICATION	HQS FILE NUMBER
8 - Unclassified			S E C R E T	DESTROY WHEN NO LONGER NEEDED

CONTINUATION OF DISPATCH	CLASSIFICATION ~~S E C R E T~~	DISPATCH SYMBOL AND NUMBER BD 5847

a. To discuss the publicity problem with liaison and friendly elite contacts (especially politicians and editors), pointing out that the Warren Commission made as thorough an investigation as humanly possible, that the charges of the critics are without serious foundation, and that further speculative discussion only plays into the hands of the opposition. Point out also that parts of the conspiracy talk appear to be deliberately generated by Communist propagandists. Urge them to use their influence to discourage unfounded and irresponsible speculation.

b. To employ propaganda assets to answer and refute the attacks of the critics. Book reviews and feature articles are particularly appropriate for this purpose. The unclassified attachments to this guidance should provide useful background material for passage to assets. Our play should point out, as applicable, that the critics are (i) wedded to theories adopted before the evidence was in, (ii) politically interested, (iii) financially interested, (iv) hasty and inaccurate in their research, or (v) infatuated with their own theories. In the course of discussions of the whole phenomenon of criticism, a useful strategy may be to single out Epstein's theory for attack, using the attached Fletcher Knebel article and Spectator piece for background. (Although Mark Lane's book is much less convincing than Epstein's and comes off badly where contested by knowledgeable critics, it is also much more difficult to answer as a whole, as one becomes lost in a morass of unrelated details.)

4. In private or media discussion not directed at any particular writer, or in attacking publications which may be yet forthcoming, the following arguments should be useful:

a. No significant new evidence has emerged which the Commission did not consider. The assassination is sometimes compared (e.g., by Joachim Joesten and Bertrand Russell) with the Dreyfus case; however, unlike that case, the attacks on the Warren Commission have produced no new evidence, no new culprits have been convincingly identified, and there is no agreement among the critics. (A better parallel, though an imperfect one, might be with the Reichstag fire of 1933, which some competent historians (Fritz Tobias, A.J.P. Taylor, D.C. Watt) now believe was set by Van der Lubbe on his own initiative, without acting for either Nazis or Communists; the Nazis tried to pin the blame on the Communists, but the latter have been much more successful in convincing the world that the Nazis were to blame.)

b. Critics usually overvalue particular items and ignore others. They tend to place more emphasis on the recollections of individual eyewitnesses (which are less reliable and more divergent -- and hence offer more hand-holds for criticism) and less on ballistic, autopsy, and photographic evidence. A close examination of the Commission's records will usually show that the conflicting eyewitness accounts are quoted out of context, or were discarded by the Commission for good and sufficient reason.

c. Conspiracy on the large scale often suggested would be impossible to conceal in the United States, esp. since informants could expect to receive large royalties, etc. Note that Robert Kennedy, Attorney General at the time and John F. Kennedy's brother, would be the last man to overlook or conceal any conspiracy. And as one reviewer pointed out, Congressman Gerald R. Ford would hardly have held his tongue for the sake of the Democratic administration, and Senator Russell would have had every political interest in exposing any misdeeds on the part of Chief Justice Warren. A conspirator moreover would hardly choose a location for a shooting where so much depended on conditions beyond his control: the route, the speed of the cars, the moving target, the risk that the assassin would be discovered. A group of wealthy conspirators could have arranged much more secure conditions.

d. Critics have often been enticed by a form of intellectual pride: they light on some theory and fall in love with it; they also scoff at the Commission because it did not always answer every question with a flat decision one way or the other. Actually, the make-up of the Commission and its staff was an excellent safeguard against over-commitment to any one theory, or against the illicit transformation of probabilities into certainties.

CONTINUATION OF DISPATCH	CLASSIFICATION ~~SECRET~~	DISPATCH SYMBOL AND NUMBER BD 5847

e. Oswald would not have been any sensible person's choice for a co-conspirator. He was a "loner," mixed-up, of questionable reliability and an unknown quantity to any professional intelligence service.

f. As to charges that the Commission's report was a rush job, it emerged three months after the deadline originally set. But to the degree that the Commission tried to speed up its reporting, this was largely due to the pressure of irresponsible speculation already appearing, in some cases coming from the same critics who, refusing to admit their errors, are now putting out new criticisms.

g. Such vague accusations as that "more than ten people have died mysteriously" can always be explained in some more natural way: e.g., the individuals concerned have for the most part died of natural causes; the Commission staff questioned 418 witnesses (the FBI interviewed far more people, conducting 25,000 interviews and reinterviews), and in such a large group, a certain number of deaths are to be expected. (When Penn Jones, one of the originators of the "ten mysterious deaths" line, appeared on television, it emerged that two of the deaths on his list were from heart attacks, one from cancer, one was from a head-on collision on a bridge, and one occurred when a driver drifted into a bridge abutment.)

5. Where possible, counter speculation by encouraging reference to the Commission's Report itself. Open-minded foreign readers should still be impressed by the care, thoroughness, objectivity and speed with which the Commission worked. Reviewers of other books might be encouraged to add to their account the idea that, checking back with the Report itself, they found it far superior to the work of its critics.

CLAYTON P. NURNAD

201-289.249

FORM 53a USE PREVIOUS EDITION.	CLASSIFICATION ~~SECRET~~	☐ CONTINUED	PAGE NO. THREE

CIA Document 1035-960
Concerning Criticism of the Warren Report
CIA Document #1035-960
RE: Concerning Criticism of the Warren Report

PSYCH

1. Our Concern. From the day of President Kennedy's assassination on, there has been speculation about the responsibility for his murder. Although this was stemmed for a time by the Warren Commission report, (which appeared at the end of September 1964), various writers have now had time to scan the Commission's published report and documents for new pretexts for questioning, and there has been a new wave of books and articles criticizing the Commission's findings. In most cases the critics have speculated as to the existence of some kind of conspiracy, and often they have implied that the Commission itself was involved. Presumably as a result of the increasing challenge to the Warren Commission's report, a public opinion poll recently indicated that 46% of the American public did not think that Oswald acted alone, while more than half of those polled thought that the Commission had left some questions unresolved. Doubtless polls abroad would show similar, or possibly more adverse results.

2. This trend of opinion is a matter of concern to the U.S. government, including our organization. The members of the Warren Commission were naturally chosen for their integrity, experience and prominence. They represented both major parties, and they and their staff were deliberately drawn from all sections of the country. Just because of the standing of the Commissioners, efforts to impugn their rectitude and wisdom tend to cast doubt on the whole leadership of American society. Moreover,

there seems to be an increasing tendency to hint that President Johnson himself, as the one person who might be said to have benefited, was in some way responsible for the assassination.

Innuendo of such seriousness affects not only the individual concerned, but also the whole reputation of the American government. Our organization itself is directly involved: among other facts, we contributed information to the investigation. Conspiracy theories have frequently thrown suspicion on our organization, for example by falsely alleging that Lee Harvey Oswald worked for us. The aim of this dispatch is to provide material countering and discrediting the claims of the conspiracy theorists, so as to inhibit the circulation of such claims in other countries. Background information is supplied in a classified section and in a number of unclassified attachments.

3. Action. We do not recommend that discussion of the assassination question be initiated where it is not already taking place. Where discussion is active [business] addresses are requested:

a. To discuss the publicity problem with liaison and friendly elite contacts (especially politicians and editors), pointing out that the Warren Commission made as thorough an investigation as humanly possible, that the charges of the critics are without serious foundation, and that further speculative discussion only plays into the hands of the opposition. Point out also that parts of the conspiracy talk appear to be deliberately generated by Communist propagandists. Urge them to use their influence to discourage unfounded and irresponsible speculation.

b. To employ propaganda assets to [negate] and refute the attacks of the critics. Book reviews and feature articles are particularly appropriate for this purpose. The unclassified attachments to this guidance should provide useful background material for passing to assets. Our ploy should point out, as applicable, that the critics are (I) wedded to theories adopted before the evidence was in, (I) politically interested, (III) financially interested, (IV) hasty and inaccurate in their research, or (V) infatuated with their own theories. In the course of discussions of the whole phenomenon of criticism, a useful strategy may be to single out Epstein's theory for attack, using the attached Fletcher [?] article and Spectator piece for background. (Although Mark Lane's book is much less convincing that Epstein's and comes off badly where confronted by knowledgeable critics, it is also much more difficult to answer as a whole, as one becomes lost in a morass of unrelated details.)

4. In private to media discussions not directed at any particular writer, or in attacking publications which may be yet forthcoming, the following arguments should be useful:

a. No significant new evidence has emerged which the Commission did not consider. The assassination is sometimes compared (e.g., by Joachim Joesten and Bertrand Russell) with the Dreyfus case; however, unlike that case, the attack on the Warren Commission have produced no new evidence, no new culprits have been convincingly identified, and there is no agreement among the critics. (A better parallel, though an imperfect one, might be with the Reichstag fire of 1933, which some competent historians (Fritz Tobias, AJ.P. Taylor, D.C. Watt) now believe was set by Vander Lubbe on his own initiative, without acting for either Nazis or Communists; the Nazis tried to pin the blame on the Communists, but the latter have been more successful in convincing the world that the Nazis were to blame.)

b. Critics usually overvalue particular items and ignore others. They tend to place more emphasis on the recollections of individual witnesses (which are less reliable and more divergent-- and hence offer more hand-holds for criticism) and less on ballistics, autopsy, and photographic evidence. A close examination of the Commission's records will usually show that the conflicting eyewitness accounts are quoted out of context, or were discarded by the Commission for good and sufficient reason.

c. Conspiracy on the large scale often suggested would be impossible to conceal in the United States, esp. since informants could expect to receive large royalties, etc. Note that Robert Kennedy, Attorney General at the time and John F. Kennedy's brother, would be the last man to overlook or conceal any conspiracy. And as one reviewer pointed out, Congressman Gerald R. Ford would hardly have held his tongue for the sake of the Democratic administration, and Senator Russell would have had every political interest in exposing any misdeeds on the part of Chief Justice Warren. A conspirator moreover would hardly choose a location for a shooting where so much depended on conditions beyond his control: the route, the speed of the cars, the moving target, the risk that the assassin would be discovered. A group of wealthy conspirators could have arranged much more secure conditions.

d. Critics have often been enticed by a form of intellectual pride: they light on some theory and fall in love with it; they also scoff at the Commission because it did not always answer every question with a flat decision one way or the other. Actually, the make-up of the Commission and its staff was an excellent safeguard against over-commitment to any one theory, or against the illicit transformation of probabilities into certainties.

e. Oswald would not have been any sensible person's choice for a co-conspirator. He was a "loner," mixed up, of questionable reliability and an unknown quantity to any professional intelligence service.

f. As to charges that the Commission's report was a rush job, it emerged three months after the deadline originally set. But to the degree that the Commission tried to speed up its reporting, this was largely due to the pressure of irresponsible speculation already appearing, in some cases coming from the same critics who, refusing to admit their errors, are now putting out new criticisms.

g. Such vague accusations as that "more than ten people have died mysteriously" can always be explained in some natural way e.g.: the individuals concerned have for the most part died of natural causes; the Commission staff questioned 418 witnesses (the FBI interviewed far more people, conduction 25,000 interviews and re interviews), and in such a large group, a certain number of deaths are to be expected. (When Penn Jones, one of the originators of the "ten mysterious deaths" line, appeared on television, it emerged that two of the deaths on his list were from heart attacks, one from cancer, one was from a head-on collision on a bridge, and one occurred when a driver drifted into a bridge abutment.)

5. Where possible, counter speculation by encouraging reference to the Commission's Report itself. Open-minded foreign readers should still be impressed by the care, thoroughness, objectivity and speed with which the Commission worked. Reviewers of other books might be encouraged to add to their account the idea that, checking back with the report itself, they found it far superior to the work of its critics.

CS Copy
4/2/67
Destroy When No Longer Needed

ABOUT DOUG VAN DORN

Doug Van Dorn has pastored the Reformed Baptist Church of Northern Colorado since 2001. He graduated from Bethel College in 1992, majoring in Marketing and minoring in Bible. He was a youth pastor for four years in Denver. He holds the Master of Divinity degree from Denver Seminary (2001).

Doug has served on councils and boards for two Baptist Associations, the current one which he helped found in 2016. The Reformed Baptist Network seeks to glorify God through fellowship and cooperation in fulfilling the Great Commission to the ends of the earth. There are currently 42 churches in this international association of churches.

Doug has co-hosted the radio show Journey's End, the Peeranormal podcast, started the Waters of Creation Publishing Company, owned two small business in Minneapolis, and has appeared on numerous podcasts and radio shows.

Married since 1994, he and Janelle are the proud parents of four beautiful young girls. Born and raised in Colorado, he has climbed all 54 of Colorado's 14,000 ft. mountains and also Mt. Rainier (WA) and Mt. Shasta (CA).

To find out more about any of these things go to:
https://www.dougvandorn.com/

The Church website is
https://rbcnc.com

Books in the Christ In All Scripture Series

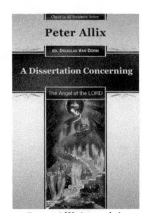

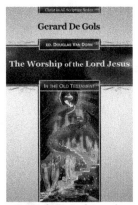

John Owen's treatment is perfect for those wanting to ground their theology of the Angel in the high orthodoxy of the Reformation. The quotations from the Fathers bolster his thesis.

Peter Allix's work is comprehensive and is especially helpful for those familiar with modern scholarship wishing to root their theology in conservative Protestant/Reformed orthodoxy.

Gerard De Gols' study, especially the second half, is imminently practical and would help anyone wanting to learn more about why it matters that Christ is present in the Old Testament.

Owen, Allix, & De Gols. The full texts together in one volume, minus quotations from the Fathers and Reformers.

The Second Edition of *From the Shadows to the Savior*, it explores even more of the titles given to Christ in the OT than Allix goes into.

Practical sermons are for the further exploration of the fullness of Christ, especially as he is found in the New Testament.

Available in Paperback or Kindle at Amazon.com

Other Books by Doug Van Dorn

Giants: Sons of the Gods

The bestselling non-fiction book on
Genesis 6 and the Nephilim.
150 reviews. 4.5+++ stars on Amazon.

Goliath. You know the story. But why is it in the Bible? Is it just to give us a little moral pick-me-up as we seek to emulate a small shepherd boy who defeated a giant? Have you ever wondered where Goliath came from? Did you know he had brothers, one with 24 fingers and toes? Did you know their ancestry is steeped in unimaginable horror? Genesis 6. The Nephilim. The first few verses of this chapter have long been the speculation of supernatural events that produced demigods and a flood that God used to destroy the whole world. The whole world remembers them. Once upon a time, all Christians knew them. But for many centuries this view was mocked, though it was the only known view at the time of the writing of the New Testament. Today, it is making a resurgence among Bible-believing scholars, and for good reason. The Nephilim were on the earth in those days, and also afterward...

This book delves deep into the dark and ancient recesses of our past to bring you rich treasures long buried. It is a carefully researched, heavily footnoted, and selectively illustrated story of the giants of the Bible. There is more here than meets the eye, much more. Here you will learn the invisible, supernatural storyline of the Bible that is always just beneath the surface, lurking like the spawn of the ancient leviathan. It is a storyline no person can afford to ignore any longer. Unlike other more sensational books on the topic, there is no undue speculation to be found here. The author is a Bible-believing Christian who refuses to use such ideas to tell you the end of the world is drawing nigh. Once you discover the truth about these fantastic creatures, you will come to see the ministry and work of Jesus Christ in a very new and exalting light. Come. Learn the fascinating, sobering, yet true story of real giants who played a significant role in the bible ... and still do so today.

Available in Paperback or Kindle at Amazon.com

The Unseen Realm: Q & A Companion
Edited by Michael Heiser.
Published by Lexham Press.

In *The Unseen Realm*, Dr. Michael S. Heiser unpacked 15 years of research while exploring what the Bible really says about the supernatural world. That book has nearly 900 reviews and a five-star rating. It is a game-changer.

Doug helps you further explore *The Unseen Realm* with a fresh perspective and an easy-to-follow format. The book summarizes key concepts and themes from Heiser's book and includes questions aimed at helping you gain a deeper understanding of the biblical author's supernatural worldview.

The format is that of a catechism: A Question followed by the Answer. There are 95 Questions (nod to Martin Luther) divided into 12 Parts:

Chapters:

**Available in Paperback or Kindle at Amazon.com
or on the Bible-software platform Logos at Logos.com**

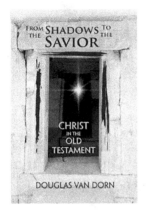

From the Shadows to the Savior:
Christ in the Old Testament

Few subjects are as important—yet ignored or misap-plied--as the one addressed in this book. Jesus Christ is the absolute center and focus of the totality of God's word. Many people confess this belief, since Jesus him-self taught it (Luke 24:27; John 5:39). Christians have done well to see this on one or two levels, yet truly un-derstanding just how primary he is as an actor—even in the Old Testament—is something few have considered.

In this book (the first edition of *Patterned, Promised, Present* in the Christ in All Scripture Series), adapted from a series of blog posts for the Decablog, Doug helps us see the light of Christ that emerges from the dark hallways of Scriptures that so many find outdated, unintelligible, and irrelevant for today's Church.

Learn how Christ is found in such things as prophecy, typology, and the law. Then, come in for a deeper study of how the Person himself is actually present, walking, speaking, and acting, beginning in the very first book of the Bible. Learn how words such as "Word," "Name," "Glory," and "Wisdom" are all ideas that the Scrip-ture itself attaches to Christ who in the OT is called The Angel of the LORD. Then see if such ideas don't radically change the way you think about all of God's word in this truly life-changing summary of Christ in the Old Testament.

Chapters:
NT Passages and Reflections
Christ in Prophecy
Christ in Typology
Christ and the Law
Christ: The Angel of the LORD
Christ: The Word of God
Christ: The Name of the LORD
Christ: The Wisdom of God
Christ: The Son of God
Christ: The Glory of God
Christ: The Right Arm of God

Available in Paperback or Kindle at Amazon.com

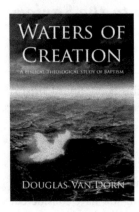

Waters of Creation:
A Biblical-Theological Study of Baptism

This is the one book on baptism that you must read. It was seven years in the making. Doug believes that until a new approach is taken, separations over the meaning, mode, and recipients of baptism will never be bridged.

This new approach traces the roots of baptism deep into the OT Scriptures. When understood properly, we discover that baptism is always the sign that God has used to initiate his people into a new creation. Baptism in the NT is not "new." Rather, it derives its origin from OT predecessors. It has a direct, sacramental counterpart, and it isn't circumcision. It is baptism. When we understand that baptism comes from baptism, especially in its sacramental expression in the priestly covenant, reasons for the NT practice begin to make perfect sense.

Now Baptists have an argument that infant Baptists can finally understand, because we are beginning our argument in the same place. This is an Old Testament covenantal approach to the Baptist position with baptistic conclusions as to the mode and recipients of baptism. That's what happens when we root baptism in baptism rather than circumcision.

Chapters:
The Baptism of Jesus
Baptism and the Sanctuary
Baptism and the Priesthood
Baptism and the Covenant
Implications for Christian Baptism

Available in Paperback or Kindle at Amazon.com

Covenant Theology:
A Reformed Baptist Primer

Douglas Van Dorn

Covenant theology is often said to be the domain of infant Baptists alone. But there really are such things as Reformed Baptists who believe in covenant theology as a basic system for approaching Scripture.

This primer sets out to give the basics of a Reformed Baptist covenant theology and to do so in a way that is understandable to the uninitiated. It was originally a series we did on Sunday nights at our church. It agrees with classical formulations of covenant theology in that there is a Covenant of Redemption, a Covenant of Works, and a Covenant of Grace in the Bible.

The book takes a multi-perspective approach to the Covenant of Redemption in that this covenant is the basis for the classic formula that Christ's death is sufficient for all, but efficient for the elect. It sees the Covenant of Works for Adam in a broader context of a covenant made with all of creation, a covenant where laws establish the parameters for creation's existence.

It differs from Paedobaptist covenant theology in that it sees the Covenant of Grace as only properly coming through Jesus Christ. OT gracious covenants are typological of the Covenant of Grace but save people on the basis of the coming work of Christ through faith alone. This is the traditional way Reformed Baptists have articulated the Covenant of Grace.

Finally, it sees an entire covenant in the Old Testament as often (but not always) missing from formulations of covenant theology. In the opinion of the author, this "priestly covenant" is vital to a proper understanding of 1. The continuity of the practice of baptism from OT to NT, 2. The answer to why we never find infants being baptized in the NT, and 3. A more precise way to parse the legal aspects of the OT economy, thereby helping us understand why the moral law continues today. This volume works from the basic presupposition that continuity in God's word is more basic than discontinuity. In this, it differs from dispensationalism and new covenant theology. The book suggests that this is the greatest strength of covenant theology, which does also recognize discontinuity.

Available in Paperback or Kindle at Amazon.com

Galatians:
A Supernatural Justification

A play on words, the subtitle of this book gives you the two main points it tries to get across. Galatians central message teaches how a person is *justified* before a holy God. This once precious and central teaching of Protestant theology is often misunderstood or relegated the pile of irrelevant, stale doctrine.

Perhaps that is why the Apostle Paul supercharges his teaching with an oft-overlooked side of this letter - the *supernatural* beings who tempt us and teach us to give up the only truth that will save us. Galatian Christians would have been familiar with these supernatural beings; their culture was steeped in it. Thus, they mistake Paul for the messenger-healer god Hermes, and Barnabas for Zeus. Paul's warning: "Even if we or an angel from heaven should preach to you a gospel contrary to the one we preached to you, let him be accursed." This is Paul's fatherly way of showing his children in the faith that the gospel is paramount; it alone is able to save. Such a warning like this can have new power, as people are returning with reckless abandon to the worship of the old gods.

This book is from a series of sermons preached at the Reformed Baptist Church of Northern Colorado in 2011.

The Five Solas
of the Reformation

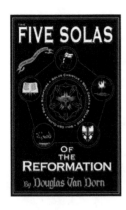

The 500th anniversary of the Reformation occurred in 2017. It was October 31, 1517 that Martin Luther nailed his 95 Thesis to the door of the great cathedral at Wittenberg, Germany. He had no idea what that simple act would do. His bold proclamation and challenge to for Rome to reform her ways and beliefs was met with hostility from some and great sympathy from others. Out of this sympathy arose Protestantism, a movement deeply concerned with grounding all things on Holy Scripture, giving glory to God alone, and recovering for that generation the biblical gospel of Jesus Christ. In five chapters, Doug Van Dorn takes us back to these ancient catch-phrases that once moved a continent. Scripture Alone, Grace Alone, Faith Alone, Christ Alone, and To God Be the Glory Alone became the rallying cry of all who longed to see men and women, boys and girls saved and set free from sin, death, and the devil. The end of the book contains four helpful Appendices on songs, Church Fathers on the solas, a bibliography for further research, and a letter from Martin Luther.

Available in Paperback or Kindle at Amazon.com

Printed in the USA
CPSIA information can be obtained
at www.ICGtesting.com
CBHW061254240924
14857CB00013B/142

9 780986 237690